The Red Army

The
Red Army

Erich Wollenberg

*Translated from the German
by Claud W. Sykes*

NEW PARK PUBLICATIONS

Published by New Park Publications Ltd.,
21b Old Town, Clapham, London SW4 0JT
1978

Re-published by kind permission of Martin Secker and Warburg Ltd.
Reproduced by offset lithography
from the first edition published in 1938

Set up, Printed and Bound
by Trade Union Labour

Distributed in the United States by:
Labor Publications Inc.,
540 West 29th Street, New York
New York 10001

ISBN 0 902030 96 5

Printed in Great Britain by
Astmoor Litho Ltd (TU),
21-22 Arkwright Road, Astmoor, Runcorn, Cheshire.

Contents

List of Maps

The Red Army

Erich Wollenberg

London
Secker & Warburg

Title page of the first English edition, published in 1938

Introduction

Few foreigners to the Soviet Union have been in a better
position than Erich Wollenberg to write about the foundation and early history of the Red Army. Despite some
political weaknesses, his book offers valuable testimony to
the character of the Red Army in its early years as well as
to its degeneration and decapitation under Stalin. The qua-
litative change it underwent in the 1930s, nowhere more
vividly described than here, is an indispensable aspect of
the rise of Stalinism. The whole previous history of the Red
Army was subsequently rewritten and distorted. The role
of its founder, Leon Trotsky, was expunged from the
record altogether, while that of Stalin and his supporters
was grossly exaggerated. A major virtue of Wollenberg's
book is that it sets the record straight on these matters.

Wollenberg himself was born into a middle-class German family in 1892. His father was a doctor and he was
studying medicine when World War I broke out. He volunteered for the imperial army and became a lieutenant. As a
front-line fighter he was wounded five times, but disgust
with the slaughter brought him into contact with the
working-class movement. In 1918 he joined the revolutionary movement which swept Germany as the Kaiser's
regime went down to defeat. He became a member of the

Independent Social Democratic Party and later of the
Communist Party of Germany (KPD). In 1918 he led a
group of Red sailors in Königsberg and he was one of the
military leaders of the short-lived Bavarian Soviet, commanding the infantry of the Dachau Army Group. Under
the name of Walter he was later one of the chief military
experts of the Communist movement in Germany and
internationally. His part in preparing for the rising of 1923
forced him to leave Germany where a court had described
him as one of the most dangerous men in the country. In
1929 he was to write *Als Rotarmist von München* descri-
bing his experiences.

In Moscow Wollenberg completed his military studies
and in turn became a Red Army instructor, coming into
close contact, as his book shows, with brilliant young commanders like Tukhachevsky who had risen to positions of
leadership during the Civil War. Evidently at this period he
was completely at one with the revolution, seeing the Russian Revolution of 1917 as only the first stage in the world
revolution, and the Red Army itself not as a national army,
but as an army at the service of the world working class.
Disillusionment set in as Stalin's policy of 'socialism in one
country' was imposed upon the Communist Party of the
Soviet Union and the Communist International as a whole.
Wollenberg could not stomach this change. He fell foul of
Stalinism and was forced to quit the Soviet Union. He was
unable to return to his native Germany where he was a
wanted man. He took refuge in France and then in North
Africa and it was there, apparently, that he linked up with
the American Forces after the landings of November 1942.
He was Press Officer for the US Army in Bavaria after
World War II and became a journalist and writer on Soviet
and military matters. Although he drifted into some dange-

rous political positions, as his book already indicates, Wollenberg remained loyal to his own past. There is no sign that he had any regrets about the part he had played as the organiser and leader of insurrection in Germany or his connection with the Red Army when it was still the army of international revolution.

From the opening pages of his book Wollenberg insists that the study of the Red Army is not an academic question but part of the preparation for revolution. In his native land he had witnessed the destruction of the old army, but only in Russia, where the revolution was successful, was it followed by the building of a new army. The conditions for this were, however, most unfavourable. The old Russian Imperial army largely disintegrated and melted away in the course of the revolution. It had been composed mainly of peasants, many of whom hastened back to their villages to take part in the seizure and redistribution of land made possible by the overthrow of Tsarism. On the side of the revolution at the outset there were only the Red Guards, formed to carry through the insurrection and protect the gains of the revolution, and the guerrilla bands of armed peasants formed to defend the land won during the revolution. From this sprang a conflict of some importance in Soviet military circles, in which guerrilla warfare was counterposed to the need for a disciplined modern army.

It was soon evident that to combat the counter-revolutionary forces based upon the old officer corps, led by professional soldiers and backed by foreign imperialism, the revolution would have to build its own army. This task was entrusted to Leon Trotsky as People's Commissar of War. Undoubtedly Trotsky was the dominating influence in the early history of the Red Army and, as Wollenberg conclusively shows, its main architect. The scale of the Civil

War and foreign intervention meant that the survival of the Soviet regime depended entirely upon the Red Army and particularly its leadership. As Trotsky saw from the start, improvisation was inevitable, making use of what material lay at hand, including military specialists from the old army not sympathetic towards the aims of the revolution.

The Red Army, Trotsky saw, had to be based upon the ideas of the worldwide socialist revolution. Like all great revolutions, the Bolshevik Revolution had to arm itself, but the Red Army, issuing from a proletarian revolution, was from the start quite different from any previous army in history. It had to create a new body of qualified officers while maintaining the closest class solidarity between all ranks. While calling upon the old military cadres who possessed knowledge of military science without which the army could not be built, everything was done to raise the level of political consciousness of the soldiers. Although Trotsky was dismissed from his post when Stalin, flanked by Zinoviev and Kamenev, assumed power after Lenin's death, down until the 1930s the Red Army continued to display many of the traits he had stamped upon it: its internationalism, its comradeship and its political consciousness. Despite all the pressure from Stalin and the bureaucracy, commanders like Tukhachevsky would never say a word publicly against their old chief.

It was ironic that the Red Army should fall under the control of Stalin, his cronies and toadies whose irresponsibility, indiscipline and tactical errors had caused it serious damage. Against the Stalinist myths, Wollenberg tells the true story of the Civil War and the Polish campaign. In the first, it was Voroshilov, backed by Stalin, whose insubordination led to the failure of the southern army around Simbirsk. According to Tukhachevsky this caused the

Civil War to be prolonged by two years. Trotsky, working
from his famous armoured train, had to take personal
charge of the operations at Sviyazhsk to retrieve the situation in the campaign brilliantly described by Larissa Reissner in an article quoted by Wollenberg. In a similar disregard for orders during the Polish campaign, the armies on
the south-western front under the command of Voroshilov
and Yegorin, with Stalin's support, disregarded orders to
march against Lublin and instead dissipated their cavalry
and other troops in a fruitless assault on Lwow. Again,
Tukhachevsky was the severest critic of this blunder which
cost the war and forced the Red Army to retreat.

Clearly, Stalin never forgot nor did he forgive Tukhachevsky, undoubtedly the most brilliant of the Red Army
commanders, for his criticisms. Stalin's revenge was
bloody: it was to cost the lives not only of Tukhachevsky
but of the leading figures of the General Staff and tens of
thousands of the best military cadres of the Soviet forces in
1938.

Wollenberg devotes a special chapter to Trotsky and the
Red Army and generally supports his views on military
doctrine. Trotsky was a determined opponent of those
who idealised guerrilla methods or who worshipped 'the
total offensive'. He saw that the Red Army had to be built
up in the most methodical way with the emphasis on training, organisation and technical efficiency as well as on
political consciousness. Although generally an admirer of
Tukhachevsky who, like himself, had come over to the side
of the revolution from the officer corps of the old army,
Wollenberg comes down decidedly on Trotsky's side over
the Polish campaign. Tukhachevsky put too much confidence in the ability of the Red Army to awaken working
class support against the Polish bourgeoisie. Trotsky was

the only member of the Central Committee to warn of the dangers of trying to carry the revolution into ethnic Poland on the point of the bayonet, and he was proved right.

Although Wollenberg supported Trotsky on military questions, he was a critic of Trotsky's political line in the 1920s and 1930s as this book shows. A word of caution is therefore necessary about his own political standpoint. Wollenberg knew at first hand of the Stalinist degeneration and his witness to its effects on the Red Army is one of the most valuable parts of this book. However, there seems little doubt that the effect of Stalinism was to disorient him politically and he lost confidence in the working class.

This tendency is still more evident in the later edition of this book to which he added several chapters on the political developments in the Soviet Union. Even in this edition he speaks of the bureaucracy as a new ruling class and he was later to adopt the view that the Soviet Union had become a state capitalist country. Wollenberg fails to defend this thesis with any convincing analysis, nor does he give any substance to his criticisms of Trotsky's policies or propose an alternative. Disillusioned with the Stalinist course during which the officers of the Red Army to whom he had been closely attached were sent wantonly to their death, he turned into an aimless commentator. This reaction is understandable, but it is not excusable. Wollenberg was better versed in military science than in Marxism.

The reader should thus be alerted to the political weaknesses and dangers of this book, which were to be demonstrated in Wollenberg's own evolution. Nevertheless it conserves considerable value as both historical evidence and personal testimony regarding the Russian Revolution and its degeneration. In its early years the Red Army was indeed an army of a new type, the product of a great revolution like Cromwell's New Model Army and the armies of the French Revolution. Unlike them it was a working class army, an army of the future. It was already showing that the proletariat was capable of mastering the most advanced military techniques necessary in the struggle against capitalism and able to make innovations of its own. To the surprise of some, they will learn that it was Trotsky and not Guderian or De Gaulle who was the first advocate of mechanised divisions. It was the Red Army, under Tukhachevsky, which first trained parachute regiments, the idea being that they would drop behind enemy lines and link up with detachments of workers fighting against their imperialist rulers.

Unfortunately the Red Army fell victim to the dead hand of the Stalinist bureaucracy. The devastation wrought in its ranks by the murder of Tukhachevsky and his companions and the mass purges of the command structure meant that when the Wehrmacht struck in June 1941, the Soviet forces had to retreat hundreds of miles and were brought to the brink of defeat. Only the resurgence during the war of the same revolutionary spirit which had animated the Red Army during the Civil War made victory possible. It was no thanks to the Voroshilovs and Budennys, Stalin's favourites, who proved to be spent forces. But once victory had been assured Stalin made sure that the army was brought strictly under control. Above all he feared that the truth would become known about the past. In the course of the political revolution against the bureaucracy the Soviet working class will have to open up all the archives and discover the truth. This book by Wollenberg is a contribution to setting history straight as far as the Red Army is concerned.

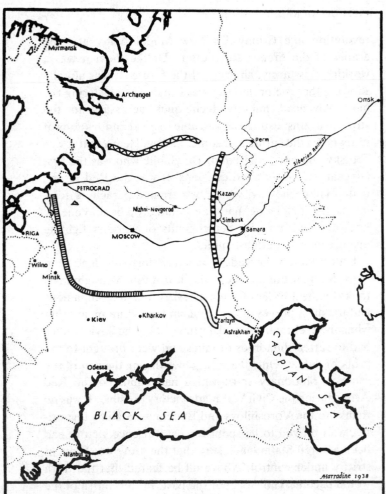

MAP I
POSITION OF THE FRONTS IN THE SUMMER OF 1918

▦▦▦▦▦▦▦	: German Army of Occupation
▭▭▭▭▭▭▭	: Don Army of the Whites under General Krasnov
▦▦▦▦▦▦▦	: Czechoslovak Legion & volunteers of the 'Konstituante'
◇◇◇◇◇◇◇	: North front of the Whites

Chapter One

In the lives of nations and classes there are moments and even whole epochs in which—so Lenin informs us—"History causes the military problem to become the essence of the political problem." Just such a period may be found in the transition stage from a capitalistic to a socialistic order of society and from an oppressed to a liberated nation.

Now the forms taken by imperialist armies are on the surface extremely manifold, and vary according to the more or less democratic or fascist forms of the various capitalistic states, but their essence remains the same. Every bourgeois army is the instrument of bourgeois dictatorship, or, to quote Lenin again, "the most ossified instrument for the maintenance of the old order of things, the strongest safeguard of bourgeois discipline, the prop of the rule of capitalism and the means of creating and inculcating a slavish obedience and keeping the masses of workers under the sway of capitalism." The transition from an imperialist to a revolutionary army and the building up of this revolutionary army are therefore tasks which must be carried

out on the basic principles laid down by the October
Revolution of 1917, no matter how details may be
varied according to the nature of that army's military
and political forms. Herein lies the great significance
which a knowledge of the origin and development of
the Red Army must possess for all socialists.

Every army reflects the political constitution and
whole order of society prevailing in the land to which
it belongs. A knowledge of the Red Army therefore,
gives us the key to a knowledge of the economic, political and social system of the Soviet Union in every
phase of its development.

Finally, international socialism must so shape its
strategy as to allow for the Red Army becoming a
decisive factor on the international battlefield. The
army is one of the most important instruments in
politics. The Red Army is the instrument of the
October Revolution, which, as Lenin the internationalist
continually emphasized, "was basically a dress rehearsal, or one of the dress rehearsals, for the proletarian world revolution." The purpose of a dress
rehearsal is to test the performances of the actors at
every point, in order to ensure the best possible effects
on the first night and eliminate as far as may be all
mistakes and weak points. The international character
of the Russian Revolution causes it to assign to the
socialistic proletariat the simultaneous rôles of critical
observer, co-operator and future actor in this dress
rehearsal, for, in Goethe's words:

"Such tasks, how well we could complete them,
If but permitted to repeat them."

In the class war for liberty great historical tasks will
be assigned not once only, but several times, and under
varying conditions. It therefore depends to a certain
extent on the workers of every land whether they can
learn from the object-lessons history affords them, so
that the task of their emancipation may be 'well completed.' Every honourable socialist, who is conscious
of his responsibilities, must study thoroughly the creation, consolidation, extension, and, alas, the degeneration of the first Soviet State and the first Red Army as
an essential condition of that completion.

Consequently all those questions which deal with the
birth, development, military strength and political trend
of the Red Army, must be considered first and foremost
by the revolutionary proletariat of all nations and the
oppressed colonial races.

The Break-Up of the Tsarist Army.

In his pamphlet *The Proletarian Revolution and the
Renegade Kautsky*, Lenin, dealing with the basic conditions necessary for the creation of a proletarian defence
force, wrote as follows:

"As Marx and Engels have frequently insisted, the
first commandment for those who would carry out a
successful revolution is to bring about the destruction
and disintegration of the old army and its replacement

by a new one. A new class of society, taking over the reins of government for the first time, can never obtain power and consolidate it without the disintegration (or, as reactionaries and cowardly philistines call it, the 'disorganization') of the old army, without enduring of necessity a difficult and painful transition stage without any army at all, and without gradually constructing, in the course of a bitter civil war, a new military organization as the defence force of the new class."

The disintegration of the old army is the essential preliminary condition for the success of any proletarian revolution; it is likewise a sign that conditions are ripe for a revolutionary seizure of power. But the causes of an army's disintegration are as manifold as the causes of a revolution, and, besides the general political, economic and social circumstances which incite to revolution, others arise from the special conditions of a military organization, such as maltreatment of soldiers, bad food and reverses in the field.

Even on the eve of the Revolution of February 1917 the Russian army was in process of complete disintegration. 19,000,000 men had by degrees been called to arms during the war years, but 'arms' was a word of only relative significance, since there were not half enough rifles for the men mobilized. For every company of 250 men in training barely a dozen rifles were available, and most of those were of an antiquated type which could not be used at the front. During instruction these rifles were passed from hand to hand; the majority of the soldiers had to practise their arms drill with dummies; frequently they were shown merely the appropriate movements. The soldier did not receive a rifle of his own until he reached a base depot, often not until he actually went into the trenches.

19,000,000 mobilized men represented about 11 per cent of Russia's entire population of 167,000,000—the country then included Finland, Poland and the Baltic States—or almost 23 per cent of the whole male population. These figures compare closely with those of the British mobilization, which put 5.7 millions of men under arms in the Great War, drawing them from a total population of 46 millions, including 22 million males, i.e. a mobilization of 12.4 per cent of the entire population or 26 per cent of the male population. Germany mobilized 13 millions out of the total population of 67.5 millions, which included 33 million males, i.e. 19 per cent of the whole population and 39 per cent of the male population.

But Tsarist Russia could not compete with the modern, highly organized industrial states. Her backwardness in industrial development, her semi-feudal agrarian classes and political constitution, her incompetent and thoroughly corrupt bureaucracy, and her insufficient and badly organized system of communications were not equal to the task of organizing, feeding and leading the millions of soldiers she mobilized. Shortage of war material began to affect the front line as early as the winter of 1914–15; in the following years the army supplies continually degenerated, while transport conditions grew steadily worse. These material factors combined with the defeats at the front (which were in part due to the defective equipment of the troops) to play an important part in the disintegration of the army. Only a small proportion of the 19 million men mobilized actually served at the front; the shortage of arms and equipment was one of the reasons why the rest had to be employed on the lines of communication and in the base area. On the eve of the October Revolution, i.e. in September 1917, a report made by General Dukhonin, the Russian Commander-in-Chief during the last days of the Kerensky régime, placed the number of deserters at about 2,000,000 while the casualty list included 1,800,000 killed, about 5,000,000 wounded and 2,000,000 prisoners. Dukhonin estimated the remaining effective strength at about 10,000,000.

The events of the revolutionary period between February and October 1917, served only to hasten the break-up of the army. Even the October Revolution could not arrest the disintegrating process; on the contrary, the fear of being overlooked in the distribution of land caused the soldiers drawn from the peasantry to desert in masses and make for their native villages. Meanwhile, their comrades from the industrial population streamed into the towns to take over the factories and help build up their class organizations.

This process of disintegration also infected the revolutionary regiments which made common cause with

the proletariat in revolt against the Kerensky régime.
According to a report on the *morale* of the 1st Brigade
of Guards drawn up by K. Yeremeyev, commander of
the Petrograd military district, to the Soviet Government on January 28, 1918, the pronouncedly counter-
revolutionary regiments, such as the Semyonov Regiment of Guards, were those least infected by the general
disintegration; in comparison with the others, and especially with the revolutionary regiments, this regiment of
Guards was the most intact of all under his command.

Brest-Litovsk.

The Soviet Government was obliged to live through
its difficult and painful period of being without an army
at the very time when the forces of German imperialism
were preparing to march on Petrograd. This was in the
days of Brest-Litovsk.

Serious differences of opinion had manifested themselves in the ranks of the Bolshevist Party. Some
members of the Central Committee were of opinion
that it was incumbent on the Soviet Government to
begin an immediate revolutionary war against German
imperialism in order to fulfil their obligations to the
Russian Revolution and the international proletariat.
This group included Bubnov, Uritsky, Lomov and
Djerjinsky, later the creator and chief of the Cheka.
Other well-known Bolshevists who championed the
same point of view were Radek, Riasonov and Piatakov.

Lenin, on the other hand, supported the tactics of the 'breathing-space,' in which the preliminary conditions essential for a revolutionary war against German imperialism were to be brought about. "If the German revolution breaks out within the next three or four weeks," he maintained, "then perhaps the tactics of an immediate revolutionary war would not destroy our socialist revolution. But supposing the German revolution does not break out within the next month? . . . The peasant troops, who are absolutely worn out by the war, would overthrow the socialist government of workers immediately after the first defeat, which would take place not after several months, but within a few weeks. Under such circumstances it would be mistaken tactics to risk the fate of the socialist revolution which has already begun in Russia. Such tactics would denote a policy of sheer adventure. But by concluding a separate peace, we shall keep our hands free for a while to continue and consolidate the socialist revolution, while at the same time we shall have leisure to create a firm economic basis for a strong Red Army of workers and peasants." This standpoint was supported in the Bolshevist Central Committee by Zinoviev, Sverdlov, Stalin, Sokolnikov, Smilga and Stassova.

Those who held to the theory of immediate revolutionary war opposed Lenin's view with the argument that the conclusion of peace would make the Soviet Government a direct agent of German imperialism. "But this argument is completely erroneous," Lenin explained, "because at the present moment a revolutionary war would make us direct agents of Anglo-French imperialism and so assist its objectives. The English have made Krylenko, our Commander-in-Chief, a direct offer of a hundred roubles a month for every Russian soldier, if we will continue hostilities. But even if we did not accept a single kopek from the French and English, we should still be giving them direct help by diverting some portion of the German army from them. In neither case can we escape from some sort of association with one or other group of imperialists."

Lenin's opinion was that it was impossible to stake the fate of the first successful proletarian revolution on the doubtful possibility of a German revolution in the near future. Nevertheless he made a practical attempt to create the conditions for an immediate revolutionary war. Getting in touch with Captain Sadoul, the member of the French Military Delegation who later became a Communist, he opened negotiations for the purpose of holding up the menacing advance of the Germans by blowing up bridges and destroying railways and rolling-stock under leadership of French officers. His decision to accept a dictated peace immediately and under any circumstances became irrevocable only when he received "the painful and shameful news that the regiments are refusing to remain in their positions or even to occupy the line of the Narva and are not carrying out the order to destroy everything on their line of retreat, to say nothing of the precipitate flight, chaos, stupidity, cowardice and slovenliness at present existing in the army."

A third group in the Central Committee of the Party, under Trotsky's leadership, represented a 'middle' point of view, which has been explained by Yoffe, Trotsky's former colleague on the Brest-Litovsk delegation and a firm supporter of his views, in his *Memoirs*. This fraction of the party cherished hopes of a German revolution and championed the continuation of the 'neither war nor peace' policy. They hoped that the German advance would in time meet with resistance; the workers and peasants, they assumed, would be moved by acts of pillage and violence on the part of the German soldiery to start guerilla warfare. The inevitable consequence of such a policy would be a revolutionization of the advancing German troops, which would then spread to the workers in Germany. These tactics, they maintained, were the only ones which could unchain the German revolution, even if their employment meant the temporary surrender of Petrograd and Moscow and a retreat to the Urals. "But if we capitulate to German imperialism and sign the peace treaty forthwith," they argued, "we commit an act tantamount to a betrayal of the German, Polish and Finnish revolutions."

During the negotiations at Brest-Litovsk in January 1918, Trotsky represented this standpoint which Yoffe has expounded, and did so in accordance with instructions from the Bolshevist Central Committee. But when the forces of German imperialism replied to his refusal to sign the dictated treaty by ordering an advance on Petrograd, Lenin's point of view won the support of the Party. An account of the final discussions in the Communist Fraction and in the general meeting of the Petrograd Soviet has been given with dramatic emphasis by L. Stupochenko, one of the Bolshevist participators in these historic sessions:

"It was on February 22, 1918, that Sverdlov opened the joint session of the two Government fractions, the Bolshevists and the Left Social Revolutionaries. He drew our attention to the fact that we had to give the Germans an answer by the following morning, and as it was already 11 p.m., he requested the speakers to be brief. Krylenko was the first to speak, but his discourse emphasized only one point: 'We have no army. The demoralized soldiers are flying panic-stricken as soon as they see a German helmet appear on the horizon, abandoning their artillery, convoys and all war material to the triumphantly advancing enemy. The Red Guards units are brushed aside like flies. We have no power to stay the enemy; only an immediate signing of the peace treaty will save us from destruction.'

"His speech was interrupted by angry interruptions from the Left Social Revolutionaries: 'That is a demagogue's trick, not the opinion of the Commander-in-Chief! Down with him!' But the Bolshevists were on Krylenko's side.

"Sverdlov had difficulty in restoring order in the meeting. The atmosphere grew white-hot. 'And where's our fleet?' came from some benches. 'Here's Comrade Raskolnikov, ask him!' replied Krylenko. Thereupon Raskolnikov, with a gesture of despair, replied from his seat: 'We have no fleet now; it is broken up. The sailors are running away to their homes and abandoning their ships to the enemy.'

"'I call upon Comrade Lenin to speak for the Bolshevist Fraction as a supporter of an immediate peace,' announced Sverdlov.

"And Lenin said: 'Yes, we are now powerless. German imperialism has gripped us by the throat, and in the west I see no proletarian fists that will deliver us from the claws of German imperialism. Give me an army of a hundred thousand men—but it must be a strong, steadfast army that will not tremble at the sight of the foe—and I will not sign the peace treaty. . . . If we retreat to the Urals, we can delay the pressure of the Germans for two or three weeks; but can you guarantee me that the world revolution will have come in a fortnight? You must sign this shameful peace in order to save the world revolution by preserving its most important and at present its only fulcrum, the Soviet Republic.'

"Since the Social Revolutionaries refused to put forward any adherent of the peace policy to speak on their behalf, Sverdlov called out: 'Bolshevists, off to the Fraction meeting!' There he opened the proceedings, and the opponents of peace overwhelmed Lenin with questions. Their onslaught was led by Steklov, who cried: 'Tell me, Comrade Lenin, what's your attitude to the clause in the treaty which forces us to withdraw all our troops from the Ukraine?'

" 'We shall fulfil our obligations by withdrawing all our troops from the Ukraine,' Lenin replied. 'But down there the devil alone knows which are Russian and which are Ukrainian soldiers. It's quite possible that there are no Russian troops at all there now—only the Ukrainian army.'

" 'Are we to let our Finnish brethren go down in a fight against odds, for want of help?'

" 'Yes, we shall bind ourselves to deny them help. But just think of that dreadful accident we had on the Finnish railways yesterday! Our railwaymen were so "careless" that they sent some trucks loaded with war material straight into Finland instead of pushing them off to the southern front. Such regrettable errors on the frontier are always possible. And as for the sailors, our Finnish comrades have asked us to recall them. They are so demoralized that they are selling their arms to the Whites, and so they are only making the fight harder for the Soviets.'

" 'But we have to bind ourselves to stop all anti-imperialist activities and give up our preparations for the world revolution!'

" 'I thought I was dealing here not with political babies, but with old members of an illegal party who know quite well how we managed to keep our activities going under Tsarism. The Kaiser is no cleverer than Nicholas.'

" 'But the party won't be allowed to print any articles against imperialism and the Kaiser in its press! That would be a breach of the Brest Treaty.'

" 'The Central Executive Committee of the Soviets and the Council of People's Commissaries will sign the treaty, but the Central Committee of the Party won't. The Soviet Government can take no responsibility for what the Party does.'

"The fraction decided by a majority to sign the treaty, making voting compulsory for all Bolshevists except the Latvian comrades, who were permitted to leave the room before it took place, since they could not be expected to take responsibility for the doom of Soviet Latvia.

"Despite the lateness of the hour—it was already 3 a.m.—a large number of people filled the benches in the assembly hall. At last the speeches were finished and the long-expected vote took place. 116 voted for peace, and 85 against, with 26 abstentions. Two anarchists refused to vote. Shouts were heard from the benches: 'Traitors! You have betrayed our country! Judases! German spies!' We filed out into the street to the accompaniment of yells, roars and cat-calls. It was six o'clock in the morning, but still dark, with only faint gleams of light in the eastern sky."

Those 'faint gleams of light' were the breathing-space

we needed to build up a socialist economic system and an army for revolutionary warfare.

The Brest episode brought the Soviet Government to the edge of an abyss. It was compelled to retreat before the advance of German capitalism without striking a single blow, because it did not possess an army equipped with all the modern instruments of war and led by men versed in the art of modern war. The weapons of criticism were impotent against the 'criticism of weapons.'

The Russian revolutionaries and friends of the Russian Socialist Revolution found themselves faced with the fearful question: Was Kautsky right in saying that "War is not the proletariat's strong point"? If he spoke truth, then the isolated Soviet Republic must fall an easy prey to the imperialist powers, unless the Great War ended with a victorious revolution of the oppressed classes. The victory of either imperialist group, or a compromise between the two, would spell its doom.

Brest-Litovsk proved how correct was Marx's prophetic assertion that "the revolution will have to fight modern instruments and arts of war with modern instruments and arts of war." But another statement of the creator of scientific socialism opines that "the bourgeoisie teaches the proletariat how to use its arms."

Could the proletariat learn the art of war under bourgeois leadership? Or would its own strength enable it to create a modern army, equipped with modern war

material which it could use to advantage? The proletarian victory of the October Revolution did not decide
this question, for it was the result of a struggle between
workers and soldiers trained by the bourgeoisie on the
one hand and the remains of the old army—then
thoroughly demoralized and in process of disintegration
—on the other. Even after Brest-Litovsk the military
problem remained the fateful problem of the Socialist
Revolution. It hung like a sword of Damocles over the
head of the youthful Soviet Government.

The Bolshevist Military Organization.

No special cadres had undergone training in pre-
revolutionary days for the task of building up an army.
The Bolshevist Party had its own illegal military organizations within the Tsarist Army, but the mission of these
military cells was the spread of revolutionary propaganda among the troops and the preparation of bases
for armed insurrection.

After the victory of the proletarian revolution the
functions of these cells underwent a change. Again and
again Lenin insisted: "Since October 25 we have
become the defenders of our country and our socialist
fatherland." But the Bolshevist military workers, who
had hitherto been "full of fiery negative and destructive
tendencies" in all army affairs, as Gussev, one of the
leaders of the Bolshevist military organization, truly
said, were now forced to execute a complete change of

front. From disorganizers of the old army they had to become organizers of the new one.

The February Revolution had already brought about a certain change in the nature of the Bolshevist military work, previously concentrated solely on negation and destruction. Its former slogan: "Turn the imperialist war into a civil war" gave way to a call to action for the preparation of armed insurrection and the seizure of the reins of government. The Bolshevist military organization created special cadres of soldiers who were heart and soul with the revolution.

The task of these cadres was no longer to undermine the authority of the officers, but rather to exercise a control over their superiors in order to prevent the creation within the 'democratic' army of 'special volunteer formations' that could fight against the revolution; they also organized revolutionary military units to prepare the armed insurrection. Since these Bolshevist military workers had another field of activity among the Red Guards formed within the factories, their work in training and leading these factory hands had given them, even before October 1917, some sort of preparation for the great task which lay before them after Brest-Litovsk.

After the February Revolution, Petrograd became the centre of Bolshevist military work. The local Bolshevist Party Committee established a special 'Military Commission' to carry on work among the troops of the Petrograd garrison. Similar commissions were formed in the Baltic Fleet and at the front.

As far back as April 1917, the Petrograd Military
Commission published a journal known as *Soldatskaya
Pravda* (*Soldiers' Truth*), which became the central organ
of the Bolshevist military workers. Other military newspapers also came into existence at the front, as, for
instance, the *Okopnaya Pravda* (*Truth of the Trenches*)
of the 12th Army, which occupied the northern sector
of the Russo–German front.

As the revolutionary crisis ripened, the work of the
military organization gradually changed from the disintegration of the old army to the organization of the
new armed forces of the revolution. On June 16 an
All-Russian Conference of Bolshevist Military organizations met at the instance of the Petrograd organization.
Delegates were sent from 500 military formations,
which included about 30,000 Bolshevists in their ranks.

The Bolshevists were most strongly represented in the
troops which went over to the revolution, i.e. those on
the northern and western fronts, in the Baltic Fleet, in
Finland, in the garrisons of Petrograd and its environs
and in Moscow. They were weakest on the Rumanian
and south-western fronts.

The conference decided that the main task of the
military organizations must be the creation of revolutionary bases within and outside the army. It established in Petrograd short courses of instruction to give
Bolshevist agitators a military training before despatch-
ing them to the troops at the front.

The military organization played a prominent part in

preparing for and directing the armed insurrection, but after the victories of October 1917, the military cells tried to arrest the disintegration of the old army and build up formations of the new army within the shell of its predecessor. But it soon became manifest that the Russian workers serving in the old army were "incapable of taking it over and making active use of it for their own purposes." The old Tsarist Army, which Kerensky tried to turn into a democratic citizen army with as little success as Ebert and Noske obtained under similar circumstances not long afterwards in Germany, or Azana and Girals obtained in Spain in 1936, simply could not be evolved into a class army of the proletariat. The system of electing officers did nothing to stop the process of disintegration. As Trotsky remarked, it had to be first reduced to atoms and dissolved into its component parts. Every soldier, workman and peasant had first to return to the place of his civilian occupation and re-enter his old workers' cell in order to emerge, new-born, to join a new army.

By means of a speedy and complete demobilization the Soviet Government imposed some sort of order upon the spontaneous homeward movement of masses of soldiers. When this demobilization was accomplished, the regular army of Tsarist days ceased to exist. Only in a few isolated instances, as for example the Latvian regiments and the 4th Cavalry Division, did the Bolshevist military workers succeed in transforming units of the old army into efficient formations of the new one.

Nevertheless, the Bolshevist cells played a great part in the organization of the new army, for, as Trotsky insists, "they were the first to make it possible for us to discover the resolute though not too numerous elements, whose value was so great in the critical moments of the revolution." During the period of the October rising they did their work as commanders and commissars of military units, while many of them were destined to become organizers of the Red Guards and the Red Army.

The Red Guards.

The Red Guards in Russia had a long revolutionary tradition. As far back as the revolutionary days of 1906 the Russian working classes formed their own fighting units in the factories, whereupon the victorious counter-revolution discovered that one of its chief tasks would have to be the disarmament of the workers and the destruction of these units. But the workers re-established their defence forces or 'Red Guards' during the February Revolution of 1917.

The development of these Red Guards was at first hindered by the fact that the Soviets were still dominated by the influence of the Menshevists and Social Revolutionaries. These parties were of opinion that the Revolution must not be allowed to destroy the framework of bourgeois democracy, for they feared that in view of Russia's backwardness and the general international situation any transformation of the democratic into a socialist revolution was bound to be disastrous. They thought this would lead to a reactionary movement and the ultimate victory of the militarist-monarchist counter-revolutionaries.

On February 28, 1917, the general meeting of the Petrograd Workers' and Soldiers' Soviets was led in a first flush of enthusiasm to vote for the establishment of a 'workers' militia.' But several days later, on March 7, the executive committee of the Soviets suspended this resolution, and issued a decree whereby the workers' militia was compelled to amalgamate with the ordinary citizen militia. The enforcement of this decree assured to the bourgeoisie the control of the unified militia, and the separate militia of the workers ceased to exist as an independent class organization of the proletariat.

The military organization of the Bolshevists, which had hitherto been mainly employed in work amongst the troops, was now quickly transformed into a directing centre for the activities of the workers' militia or Red Guards. The first period of the Red Guards' illegal existence is described by M. G. Fleer, a prominent member of the Petrograd military organization:

"The Red Guard organizations which were not in close contact with the party, such for example, as the armed workers' units in the factories, were comparatively easy to camouflage, for they needed only to play the part of factory militia formations officially entrusted with the task of defending the factory buildings. These legal duties gave the workers' militia scope for much

activity. We must not forget that the factories were glad
to pay for the maintenance of this factory militia before
becoming aware of its real nature, since they felt themselves safer under the protection of their 'own' workers
than under that of the citizen militia, which could not
enforce any authority over the factory hands. The proletarian factory militias soon became a general and
inevitable phenomenon in the factories of Petrograd,
Moscow, and all other centres of Russian industry."

All the attempts made by the Provisional Government
to disarm the workers failed, and led only to a rapid
decrease of the influence wielded in the factories by the
Right Social Revolutionaries and Menshevists who
supported these efforts. Consequently the Soviet of the
Viborg quarter of Petrograd, which was, so to speak, the
workers' stronghold, unanimously decided at the end of
April to press for the formation of separate Red Guard
units, deeming this to be an indispensable task of the
proletariat. A similar resolution was passed by the
General Council of Petrograd Factory Workers which
the Bolshevist military organization had called into
existence. Both these bodies defined the aims and
objects of the Red Guard as the following:

Defence of the gains of the Revolution (gains made
by the working classes, according to the definition of the
Viborg Soviet) and defence against counter-revolutionary plots (by the ruling classes, in the words of the
Viborg Soviet).

The *Petrograd Workers' and Soldiers' Soviet News*, the

Executive Committee's official organ, on April 28, opposed the Viborg resolution in a leading article, and implored the workers "not to tread this dangerous path which threatened to break the unity of the revolutionary front." It characterized the Red Guard as a wedge driven between the revolutionary proletariat and the army, hinting that such an organization would give the enemy only too good an opportunity to persuade the soldiers that the workers were arming against them.

The situation underwent no radical change until the time of the Kornilov *putsch*. After the suppression of the Petrograd July revolt the military reactionaries breathed more freely. The Provisional Government had issued warrants for the arrest of the Bolshevist leaders on account of their participation in the revolt; Lenin and Zinoviev were in hiding in Finland, whilst Trotsky and Kamenev were in prison. The working classes were in a state of depression.

Then, one day towards the end of August, General Kornilov, Commander-in-Chief at the front, marched on Petrograd, with the intention of overthrowing Kerensky's Provisional Government and establishing a military dictatorship as a transition stage to the restoration of the monarchy. Events followed one another at a breathless pace.

The Provisional Government was compelled to seek help from the workers. The Red Guard emerged from the twilight of its semi-legality and was armed. The entire defence of Petrograd and the immediate fight against Kornilov were almost exclusively in its hands. On August 28 a session of the Petrograd Workers' and Soldiers' Delegates decreed the immediate establishment of a Workers' Militia and the registration of all revolutionary workers for the armed defence of the capital.

Within a few days 25,000 workers enrolled in the militia. The Red Guards, who were known in Petrograd as the Workers' Militia, became the official armed force of the Petrograd Soviet, in which the Bolshevists had now obtained a majority. The leadership of this Petrograd Soviet was then in the hands of the Bolshevist representative, L. D. Trotsky, who had acted as its vice-president as far back as the revolutionary years 1905–6.

The Red Guards then gave themselves a constitution of a purely military nature, which divided them into decads, corporals' squads, companies, etc., along with special technical units, such as dynamiters, cyclists, telegraphists, machine-gunners, artillerymen, and so on. The smallest fighting unit of the Red Guard was the decad, which consisted of 13 men. Four decads formed a corporal's squad (53 men), three corporals' squads a company (160 men), three companies a battalion, consisting of 480 men, plus technical units which made the total strength from 500 to 600; all the battalions of a district formed the district division, which, if numerous enough, was subdivided into regiments. After the Kornilov *putsch* the Red Guards in Moscow and the other Russian industrial centres were legalized and armed by the same procedure as in Petrograd.

The Red Guard made feverish preparations for an armed insurrection. Podvoisky, who served on its staff, writes as follows:

"When the Kornilov adventure was over, our next task was to see that the arms remained in the hands of the workers and so create an armed force which we could use to seize the reins of government. In the military organization of the Bolshevists we found cadres of instructors, whom we employed in the factories. Thus a close, purposeful military network, built up by us according to plan, came into existence. The further growth of the proletariat's armed forces compelled us to initiate courses of instruction, in which our comrades who had served as non-commissioned officers could extend their military knowledge and prepare themselves to work as instructors."

But the Kerensky Government did not suspend operations against the Red Guard, that is, against armed class organizations of the proletariat, when the Kornilov danger was over. On September 5 the military Governor-General of Petrograd issued an order requiring all firearms to be registered by September 30. The Red Guard took no notice of this order, and on September 21 Nikitin, the Menshevist Minister of the Interior, issued the following decree:

"The Red Guard organizations are to be kept under permanent observation. After consultation with the

Commander-in-Chief, measures will be taken to disarm
the Red Guard in view of their liability to undertake
criminal activities. The registration of arms is to be
undertaken by the militia.[1] The regulations dealing with
the carrying of arms are to be examined, and a bill must
be brought in to tighten up the penalties for un-
authorized carrying of arms."

The Menshevists carried on a violent propaganda
campaign for the purpose of playing off the regular
troops against the armed workers. At a general meeting
of the Soviets of soldiers' delegates held in Moscow on
October 5 they handed in a resolution which, after
referring to the great services rendered by the army to
the Revolution, went on to state that "as a class army
the Red Guard is a danger to the cause of the Revolution; since we now possess a revolutionary army, it is
harmful because it forms an opposition to the national
army, thus dividing the forces of democracy and giving
the enemies of the Revolution opportunity to sow dis-
cord between one part of it and another, which must
undoubtedly lead to the weakening of revolutionary
democracy as a whole."

This resolution was not passed, but the soldiers'
delegates, who had remained in office ever since the
February Revolution, took up an attitude hostile to the
Red Guard and sabotaged the work of arming them.
The rank and file of the army were of a different
opinion, however, as we may see from the following

---

[1] I.e., the citizen police.

soldiers' resolution, issued in the *Social Democrat* of October 12:

"Do not believe those liars who tell you that the creation of the Red Guard means a campaign against the soldiers. Nothing must be allowed to separate the soldiers from the workmen. They must stand together."

In the October fighting the Red Guards and revolutionary units of the regular army amalgamated for the time to form an armed force that could act homogeneously on behalf of the proletarian revolt. When the revolutionary soldiers went back to their units after the victory and there demobilized themselves in order to return to their factories or villages, they left the Red Guard to act as armed defence forces for the factories and so constitute the picked troops of the Revolution. The fighting value of the various Red Guard formations was by no means uniform, as it depended on the strength of their Bolshevist cadres, the extent to which they were permeated with experienced soldiers from the front, and the personal and military qualities of the men they elected as leaders.

The principle of the election of officers was universally established. From the standpoint of military qualifications, this was bound to affect the efficiency of the units to a greater or less degree. The Red Guardsmen set less store by the standard of military capacity in their commanders than by the soundness of their political views, and were, indeed, often moved to vote for candidates who enjoyed universal popularity. This often led to currying favour and to demagogic tricks and intrigues.

The Red Guards were equal to their task of defending the new Soviet régime until the counter-revolutionaries coalesced and sent properly organized troops against them. But the Guards, mainly drawn from the towns and industrial centres, were found wanting as a defence for the dictatorship of the proletariat when called upon to face attacks by White armies consisting of regulars. Yet, as the Historical Section of the War Academy notes, they acted in the first months of the Civil War as "the shield of the Russian proletariat against the enemy operations of foreign and native counter-revolutionaries. Using them as a basis, the Soviet régime began to build up its armed forces, and the first fighting formations of the Red Army were grouped round the Red Guard divisions."

Guerilla Warfare.

While the Red Guards were in process of formation in the industrial centres, another force of unique character came into existence spontaneously in the steppe lands. This was the guerillas or bands of armed peasants who formed units to defend the land they had won in the October Revolution. The special character of Russian guerilla warfare was determined by the following factors:

The immense size of Russia and her comparatively

scanty population; the defective system of transport and communication, which underwent further degeneration in the course of foreign and civil war; the lack of reliable contact with the capital; the extraordinary diversity of social structure, culture, density of population and national composition in the peasantry, and finally the diverse nature of the country, i.e. steppes, mountains and *taiga* (Siberian virgin forest).

Speaking generally, we find that the guerilla movement assumed two widely contrasted aspects, represented respectively by the Ukrainian guerillas, among whom the influence of the individualistic wealthier peasants predominated, and the Siberian guerillas, who manifested the peasant-proletarian disciplined character of the movement. Naturally the line dividing these two opposites was by no means a territorial one; indeed, both these guerilla manifestations often existed side by side, and were often closely woven with one another in the same band.

The greater organizational capacity and better discipline of the Siberian bands was to some extent due to social conditions, but mainly to the immense distances of the Siberian steppes and *taiga*, which force men to depend one upon another and to afford mutual assistance in the battle against Nature. Moreover, for more than a century Siberia had been the land to which the Tsars banished political opponents who were inconvenient to them; for generations these exiles had contrived to raise the revolutionary consciousness of the

entire Siberian population, including the peasantry, to
an extraordinarily high level. We may follow the
development of one of these Siberian guerilla bands,
typical of many others, in the writings of Ilyukov, who
organized and led the guerillas of Sutshan:

"The workers alone came forward as defenders of the
Revolution during the period of the landing of the army
of intervention at Vladivostok and the operations
against the Czechoslovak legionaries. The majority of
the broad masses of peasantry remained inactive. The
revolutionary forces of the peasantry did not develop
until four or five months later, i.e. at a time when all
Siberia and the Far East was in the hands of the White
Guards. Uncurbed reaction took possession of the
towns, but when the counter-revolutionaries established
their power by fire and sword, the peasantry gradually
began to fathom the true significance of the events
which were taking place.

"The rule of the Whites revealed itself as an excellent
means for revolutionizing, in the course of a few
months, not only the villages, but also the petty bourgeoisie and intelligentsia of the towns. The peasants of
the Sutshan district assembled and formed a 'Committee
to organize revolutionary resistance to the counter-
revolutionaries and interventionists.' Ilyukov was
elected president. Soon further bands were formed in
neighbouring villages.

"The committee proposed to occupy the whole of the
Sutshan valley and establish contact with the Sutshan

coal-mines and railway in order to form further workers'
organizations there; but the subsequent course of
events gave them no chance to complete their plans.
The news from the front was ever more favourable for
the Whites, while the Red Guard retreated and suffered
one defeat after another. We were compelled to begin
an immediate offensive in order to divert as many of the
enemy's forces as possible to ourselves and away from
the Ural front.

"None of us then believed that our revolt would lead
to an immediate seizure of power. On the contrary, we
all prepared for a long, weary, obstinate war, which
could not assume the character of regular warfare, but
must be fought out as a *franc-tireur* campaign, the kind
of war which was the easiest for us to wage and which
would nevertheless hit the enemy at his most vulnerable
points. On December 21 the leaders of the various
fighting formations held a conference at the village of
Frolovka, and decided to start the revolt immediately
and to impose taxes on the wealthy peasants in order to
secure the sinews of war."

At first the guerilla bands provisioned themselves
from the food they found in the villages, but in course
of time they established their rule over compact areas of
guerilla territory which made them independent of the
'peasants' larders' by opening up more or less constant
sources of supply from the forest revenues, from the
territory they occupied, and from the taxes laid on the
wealthy peasants.

The Siberian guerilla bands worked in close touch with the workers of the towns, from whom they received financial assistance. They envisaged their task as the disorganization and destruction of the enemy's lines of communication. They did incalculable damage to Admiral Kolchak and prepared the ultimate victory of the Red Army. Many guerilla bands even took the initiative in organizing the workers for the revolutionary conflict. The 'Staff of the Revolutionary Guerilla Bands of the Sutshan Valley,' for instance, issued on February 2, 1919, the following appeal to the workers of Vladivostok:

"Workers and comrades! A conflagration which must spread to all honourable workers and a revolt of the oppressed masses have broken out in Sutshan like the mighty blaze that may arise from the striking of a single match. This revolutionary flame, which has burnt up the whole of the outworn world of yesterday that stood in its path, has also caught the peasantry. The spirit of revolution, kept down by centuries of oppression and by the landed proprietors and capitalists, has lived and thrived among the peasantry. To us, worker comrades! Join our army! Rise up to fight for the Revolution of Workers and Peasants! Long live the World Revolution! Long live the power of the Soviets!"

This appeal glows with the pathos which generations of banished revolutionaries, beginning with the Decabrists and ending with the Narodniks and Bolshevists, had planted in the hearts and minds of the Siberian people.

The strength of the Siberian guerilla bands lay in their intimate knowledge of the *taiga*, but neither courage nor numerical superiority availed them when involved in open warfare against well-trained, well-armed opponents. When guerilla bands with a total strength of about 30,000 men quitted the shelter of the virgin forest in the spring of 1920 and advanced against the towns of the Amur district, they fell victims to a Japanese onslaught on the night of April 4–5. They were unable to withstand forces they outnumbered by three to one when fighting on unaccustomed terrain.

It is only natural therefore that we should find gratitude to the sheltering *taiga* running like a red thread through countless songs of these guerilla bands:

> "Sombre Taiga, danger-ridden,
> Massed, impenetrable trees!
> Yet we rebels, safely hidden
> In thy glades, found rest and ease.
>
> Life and liberty we owe thee,
> Strength to fight another day.
> So our gratitude we'll show thee
> In the homage of this lay."

In addition to the revolutionary-proletarian guerillas, there were other bands in Siberia in which the influence of the wealthier peasants predominated. There were, in fact, guerilla bands in which many shades of opinion were represented, including those typical of the Ukraine, and eventually destined to become a source of serious danger to the Proletarian Revolution there.

The Ukraine was the only area in European Russia in which guerilla warfare developed into a mass manifestation and assumed dimensions unparalleled in history. On the other hand, the guerilla movement north and east of the Volga proceeded on lines very similar to those which characterized it in Siberia. When these bands acted independently, they did excellent work, but they were unable to fit into the framework of a regular army, in which there was constant friction between them and the other troops. K. Yeremeyev, who organized the first corps of Red Volunteers when commanding the Petrograd military district in the autumn of 1918, has given us the following account of his experiences with guerilla bands:

"The sailors belonging to the Baltic Fleet and several guerilla contingents preceded the 1st Corps to the front. The guerilla bands contained pugnacious, enthusiastic men who could not endure all the preliminary operations and wanted to go into action at once. We certainly had a lot of trouble with them at the front. They often upset all our plans and arrangements; they never conformed to any general scheme, but just trusted to their own inspiration. The "Wolf Pack" band did specially good work; it was commanded by a sailor, and consisted entirely of sailors, soldiers and workmen. An anarchist band also distinguished itself; it was not a particularly large one—barely two hundred men, but a very compact body, firmly knit together by the reckless courage of all its members. Both these bands were recalled from the front and placed at my immediate disposal; we sent them to Finland, where Whites and Germans were advancing against us. Almost all the members of both bands met their deaths there, but they fought valiantly and inflicted great losses on the Whites."

The thickly populated Ukraine, with its ancient culture and its class and racial antagonisms, was the birthplace of the anarchist guerilla bands. that were hostile to any form of centralization. But the chief characteristic of the Ukrainian guerillas was their fickleness. Sometimes they allied themselves with the Red Army, but at any moment they were liable to declare their neutrality or to go over to the Whites. Lenin has left us the following commentary on the guerilla warfare in the Ukraine, which I quote from a speech he made in the Moscow Soviet on July 4, 1919:

"The original guerilla bands in the Ukraine were brought into existence by the very insufficient class-consciousness there, the general inefficiency and lack of organization, and the disorganization caused by Petliura. The peasants simply took up arms, chose an *ataman* (captain) and instituted a government of their own there and then. They paid no heed to any central power, and each Ukrainian *ataman* thought he could solve all his country's problems without bothering about events in the capital. We must dread the guerilla movement, the arbitrary behaviour of the individual bands and their disobedience to authority; we must dread them like fire, for they will lead to our destruction."

When the French and Greek troops of the army of intervention in Southern Russia occupied the Black Sea ports, the guerilla chief Grigoriev attacked them and forced them to evacuate these towns in precipitate haste. But shortly afterwards Grigoriev started a revolt against the Soviet authority which shook the Red Army's entire southern front. The largest Ukrainian guerilla band, which was commanded by Makhno, then formed a military alliance with the Red Army against General Denikin.

Though Makhno's guerillas played a decisive part in the defeat of Denikin, it was not long before Makhno turned against the Red Army. The result of the ancient national hatred of the oppressors from Great Russia was that the Ukrainian peasants preferred to be under the leadership of their 'own' peasant farmers, large and small, rather than to take orders from the Ukrainian proletariat, which 'had made common cause with Great Russia.' A still more cogent reason for the fickleness of the Ukrainian guerilla bands was the rigorous way in which all agricultural produce was requisitioned for the needs of the Red Army.

In addition to the political guerilla movement in the Ukraine, we may note the development of a unique form of banditry, which was in part complementary to it. A veritable army of deserters from both the hosts opposing one another in civil warfare gathered together in the woods and formed a kind of third party, which they called the 'Greens,' taking their name from the colour of the woods that sheltered them. Bands of these Greens instituted plundering expeditions in order to procure the supplies they needed, thus contributing largely to the general disorganization and prejudice against the political guerilla movement.

The great majority of the Greens, however, were merely the result and expression of the peasantry's fickleness. When at length the peasants were moved by their experience of both Reds and Whites to come in on the side of the Soviet Government, the deserters emerged from their woods and joined the Red Army of their own accord.

Trotsky often attended mass meetings of these men, whom he addressed as "Deserter Comrades." In the summer of 1919, a report made to the Moscow Soviet on the change of front that was becoming noticeable in the ranks of the Green deserter bands, said:

"Trotsky has travelled through many districts in which we formerly strove against the deserters in vain. He has spoken at their meetings, where he found among them at least 10,000 men who had been easily intimidated or all too easily defeated by the bourgeoisie. He told me of the change that had taken place in these men's views, which is indeed indescribable. Some commissaries say that we are being veritably swamped by the stream of former deserters now pouring into the Red Army."

The days of successful guerilla warfare came to an
end when the Civil War exchanged small operations for
large ones on entrenched fronts. "The guerilla movement," wrote Trotsky in 1923 in a work on the Red
Army, "was a necessary and adequate weapon in the
first period of the Civil War. The fight against the
counter-revolution, which had not yet found itself and
could put no compact armed masses into the field, was
waged with the assistance of small, independent bodies
of troops. This kind of warfare demanded self-sacrifice,
initiative and independence. But as the war grew in
scope, it gradually came to need proper organization
and discipline. The guerilla movement then began to
turn its negative pole towards the Revolution."

The transfer of the guerilla bands to the regular Red
Army was attended with considerable difficulties. A
number of bands which refused to conform to the central
Soviet authority were forcibly liquidated. Among them
was the Ukrainian guerilla army commanded by 'Papa
Makhno.' But other guerilla bands, including those led
by Chapayev and Budyonny, gradually took their
places in the Red Army's ranks, after much vacillation
and resistance. There was, indeed, a temporary and
intermediate stage of 'regular guerillas,' in which
guerilla bands fought side by side with the Red Army
formations, under a common leader and with a unified
plan of operations.

The suppression of the guerilla movement was
rendered all the more difficult by the fact that guerilla

tendencies began to manifest themselves inside the Red Army, even infecting Communists, especially those of peasant origin; many old soldiers and non-commissioned officers also succumbed to them.

Among the Communists who introduced guerilla tendencies into the Red Army was Klim Voroshilov, the Bolshevist of 1905 and Tsarist volunteer in the Great War. Under his leadership a special group came into existence in the Red Army, known as the N.C.O. Clique, because it was composed almost entirely of former non-commissioned officers. Their opposition to the centralized army authorities, and more especially to the employment of military specialists, often took extreme forms, such as a decision to ignore all commands issued by former Tsarist officers.

This decision was their answer to the appointment of the young Lieutenant of the Tsarist Guards, Tuchachevsky, to the command of the First Red Army. On June 2, 1918, by order of the Revolutionary Council of War and the Soviet Government, he proclaimed the mobilization of all former officers, who were thus called up for service with the Red Army. Loud threats to shoot the 'Guards Officer' were uttered by members of Voroshilov's clique, whereupon Trotsky issued an order, countersigned by Lenin, to the effect that insubordination against officers appointed by the Revolutionary Council of War would be punished with the utmost severity.

Although the guerilla tendencies of the N.C.O. clique

were no longer manifested so openly, opposition to Lenin's and Trotsky's conception of the Red Army did not cease. The points at issue may be summarized as follows :

(1) The supporters of the guerilla point of view opposed compulsory military service and favoured the voluntary system.

(2) They were against the appointment of officers and in favour of their election.

(3) They were against the appointment of Tsarist officers and in favour of the principle that all army orders should be discussed and approved by the troops before being carried out.

The following standpoint was also supported in theory by Voroshilov and his friends:

A centralized army is the institution of an imperialist state. The Revolution must live up to itself by abolishing once and for all trench warfare and the centralized army. Small irregular operations are the true tactics of the revolution.

The fundamental error of the adherents of guerilla warfare was that they carried their 'theory of revolutionary warfare' to the pitch of trying to apply their organizational forms and fighting tactics to situations entirely different from those which had rendered them necessary, or at any rate inevitable, for armed proletarian units at a certain stage in the development of the class war.

The Construction of the New Army.

On January 12, 1918, the Council of People's Commissars issued a decree concerning the 'formation of the socialist army,' which was to be 'built up from below on the principles of election of officers and mutual comradely discipline and respect.' The purpose of this army was defined as follows:

"The old army functioned as an instrument for the oppression of the workers by the bourgeoisie. With the transfer of state authority to the workers and exploited classes there arose a need for a new army, to serve as a bulwark for the Soviet régime at the present time, a groundwork for the replacement in the near future of the standing army by the armed force of the people, and a basis for the Socialist Revolution in Europe."

For the moment this decree existed merely on paper. The first formations of the Red Army were not raised until February 23, 1918, when the forces of German imperialism were marching on Petrograd, so that this date may be termed the birthday of the Red Army of Workmen and Peasants. At the same time the Central Comittee of the Bolshevist Party and the Central Executive Committee of the Soviets passed resolutions appointing L. Trotsky People's Commissar for War and entrusting him with the task of organizing and directing the armed forces of the dictatorship of the proletariat at the moment of the new Soviet Government's greatest danger.

The voluntary principle was for the moment allowed to remain. Conscription could not be applied until the ideological and organizational conditions essential for its enforcement had crystallized. These were: (1) A change of mood in the peasantry, who were indescribably war-weary. (2) The creation of administrative machinery in the capital and provinces to deal with the men called to the colours.

On April 22 the Soviet Government published a decree providing for 'universal military training.' This training was to take place in the factories and other places of production, and generally outside working hours. Volunteers were under an obligation to serve for six months.

On May 10 the Red Volunteer Army numbered 306,000 men. 34,000 of the 50,000 Red Guards were taken into the new army, while the other volunteers were drawn mainly from the men of the old army and fleet.

On June 12 the Soviet Union mobilized the first five classes (1892–7) in fifty-one districts of the Volga area, the western area of European Russia, and Siberia, i.e. in all districts immediately menaced by internal or external counter-revolutionaries. At the end of July 1918, two classes were successfully mobilized in Moscow and Petrograd. In July, the Fifth Soviet Congress approved this mobilization as an emergency measure, and accepted the conscription plan brought forward by the Council of People's Commissars. But until well into

1919 this compulsory mobilization was supplemented by appeals to members of various social organizations to enlist for voluntary service.

Thus we find appeals from the factory managements to the workers, from the Poor Peasants' Committees to the Peasants, and from the Trade Unions and the Communist Party to their members. These last were more or less of a compulsory nature, since refusal to respond implied expulsion from the bodies whose authority backed up the appeals. Up to October 1, 1919, about 180,000 members of the Party enlisted, while 75 per cent of the refusals to serve came from the peasantry.

There were also figures which revealed desertions of 5 to 7 per cent of the troops at the front. The total number of deserters during the winter of 1919–20 was 2,846,000, of whom 1,543,000 returned to duty voluntarily when the Soviet Government guaranteed them immunity from punishment.

Only a part of the men called to the colours could be armed; the personnel registers of the Red Army were therefore divided into the two categories of 'eaters' and 'fighters.' The figures of the Red Army for its first two years were:

End of 1918	. .	600,000 'eaters'
Feb. 1, 1919	. .	1,000,000 'eaters'
Jan. 1, 1920	. .	3,000,000 'eaters'
Oct. 1, 1920	. .	5,498,000 'eaters'

But at the period when its numbers were greatest, i.e. in the autumn of 1920, the Red Army did not possess more than 400,000–500,000 rifles and swords. The unarmed men did not belong to the 'Labour Army' which was raised in 1919 after the liquidation of several fronts, but were drafted into units allotted to the formations in which the armed men served. In October, 1920, the 5,490,000 'eaters' were distributed as follows:

> 2,600,000 in the districts under military control
> 159,000 in the Labour Army
> 391,000 in the Reserve Army
> 1,780,000 at the front.

The remainder, amounting to half a million, were assigned to office, guard, railway and transport duties. When the Polish front came into existence in the same year, it absorbed only 150,000 'fighters' to 600,000 'eaters,' so that there were four soldiers behind every one in the front line.

This disproportion between the armed and unarmed men in the Red Army was mainly due to the complete breakdown of industry and agriculture, the enormous transport distances, and the fight against banditry, which necessitated the retention of military formations—even if unarmed or only semi-armed—to occupy and patrol the hinterland and turn it into a supply basis for the army.

The forces at the front were almost entirely self-supporting. In view of the breakdown of the transport system this state of things was a necessity, but it served to accentuate the differences between workers and peasants, and that unfortunately at the most vulnerable spots, i.e. immediately behind the fronts and on the lines of communication, which generally extended to a length of over 200 kilometres. This fact that the Red Army was compelled to live on the country was one of the causes of the extreme vacillations among the peasantry and their independent guerilla bands.

The troops at the front were not merely self-supporting in the matter of rations, and partially, indeed, in the matter of equipment, but they also found it necessary to organize and build up their formations in the front area, where to a certain extent they were self-supporting in the matter of the man-power needed to fill the gaps in their ranks. This creation of a revolutionary army practically 'under enemy fire' is depicted most vividly by S. I. Gussev in his work, *The Lessons of the Civil War:*

"Time no longer permitted us to raise formations anywhere in the hinterland. All volunteers and conscripts were of necessity allotted to the troops at the front, especially at the beginning of the Civil War. Battalions swelled into regiments; weak regiments were amalgamated, divisions were formed of single regiments. At the front we did not merely fight battles; we had to undertake terrific organizational work there as well. Behind the front line special reserve armies came into existence, and were assigned the task of giving military and political training to the man-power drawn from the hinterland. Perhaps the most characteristic feature of the Red Army (which indeed distinguishes it from all former armies) was the fact that two-thirds of its regular troops were raised, or at least finally equipped, directly by the front command and not by the All-Russian Military Centre in the hinterland.

"The work of the General Staff was limited to mobilization and the collection of statistics. Despite every effort, the attempt to raise a Red Army by means of powerful central administrative machinery broke down at the very beginning. The reverse took place, for the Red Army was raised by absolutely decentralized machinery. Individual formations came into existence in local sectors of the front, and then gradually amalgamated to form a centralized army. The creation of the Red Army by means of powerful centralized machinery is therefore impossible, because this powerful centre does not exist. The military machine of a proletarian state is always weak at the beginning. It is disastrous to try to carry out centralization unless you possess a powerful centre."

For this reason, says Trotsky, "all regiments were in themselves living improvisations, and the army as a whole was one also. For our task of constructing the Red Army we had to exploit Red Guard formations and regiments of the Tsarist Army, peasant leaders and Tsarist generals. In fact, we created the army out of all the historical materials at our disposal, and did our work from the point of view of a proletarian state fighting for its existence, consolidation and development."

The multifarious elements characteristic of the first

phase of the armed forces of the revolution—multifarious in respect of their military organization, form of armament, and fighting methods, and multiform in respect of their nationalities and ideologies—were welded together in the melting-pot of the four years of civil war and the Polish campaign into a homogeneous Red Army of workers and peasants.

Chapter Two

Historical Parallels.
                              Every great revolution has
been forced, in the course of a civil war and a national
war of independence, to create a new revolutionary
army as it were out of the ground and on the debris of
the old army—the army of the rulers and oppressors.
If the revolutionary class or party failed in this military
task, if it could not gain the breathing-space it needed
in order to hold on through the painful army-less period
of transition, it had failed in the problem set it by
history and was doomed to sink back for a long period
of further development (or, perhaps, for ever) into the
void where history has nothing to record.

In the German Peasants' War, which broke out in
the spring of 1525 with the suddenness of a thunderstorm, the peasants, as soon as they were left in the
lurch by the citizens of the towns, wasted their strength,
and so suffered defeat by the armies of the nobility,
although they had the 'big battalions' on their side.
They did not know how to weld their scattered detachments of armed men into an army; they were unable to
solve the problem of military leadership. The centuries

of misery that followed in Germany, and the manifestations of Hitler's barbarism, may be ultimately traced to the fact that the Peasants' Revolt (the most important preliminary condition for a civic revolution) failed to give the 'military arguments' a satisfactory answer.

The great rise of the English bourgeoisie in the last few centuries is due to the fact that Cromwell was his own sword as well as his own ideologist. He organized the army of the Long Parliament and was able to lead it to victory.

Like the October Revolution, the French Revolution was exposed to furious onslaughts from internal foes and interventionist armies, during its 'painful army-less period.' It had to improvise its own revolutionary armies at the front. It soldiers were as ill-fed and ill-trained as the men of the Red Army; their garments were as ragged, their equipment at the front as bad. They were the butt of politicians and military writers, who asked: "What sort of soldiers are these? A collection of tramps, beggars and bandits!" But these beggars, these bare-footed *sans-culotte* warriors defeated the splendidly equipped armies the rulers of Europe sent against them. A contemporary Winston Churchill would have been able to speak of the "Fourteen and more kings" with the same self-satisfaction that his modern successor displayed in 1919 when he boasted of the "Fourteen States" fighting against the October Revolution.

The creation of a revolutionary army amid foreign and civil war is therefore no new problem imposed by history for the first time on a revolutionary class or party. Nevertheless, Lenin had right on his side when, in the course of his speech on March 18, 1919, at the 8th Party Day of the Bolshevist Party, he emphasized the fact that "the problem of creating a Red Army was quite a new one. Hitherto it has never made even a theoretical appearance. As Comrade Trotsky has said, we had to experiment and make trials. We attempted to carry out our mission on a larger scale than anyone else in the world has ever attempted."

What is the novelty in this creation of a Red Army on a scale unprecedented in history? It is to be found in the special class basis of the proletariat, which was not merely exploited and oppressed politically by the ruling classes, but also disinherited by them.

The feudal lords yielded up to the bourgeoisie some considerable time before their political fall their monopoly of education—or at least the monopoly they possessed by reason of their close contact with the monasteries and secular clergy; but after seizing political power and 'expropriating the expropriators' in the economic sphere, the proletariat still remained in the state of disinheritance that had been imposed on it by the vanquished bourgeoisie in the intellectual sphere, in the spheres of ability and knowledge, in the sphere of culture.

This intellectual dependence was greatest in the

period immediately following the seizure of power, that is, in the years when the bourgeoisie made their bitterest and fiercest efforts to regain their lost authority. A bankers' monopoly can be broken in a few weeks or even hours, but an educational monopoly can be overcome only by the work of years or even decades, and then only by hard, unremitting toil. Meanwhile the proletariat can count on no other teachers save the specialists who have hitherto served the bourgeoisie. This rule holds good for all branches of knowledge, and most especially for military knowledge.

The first great but groping attempt of a proletariat to seize and maintain political power was the experiment of the Paris Commune. The military problem was not one of the least causes of its failure. In his historical work *The Paris Commune*, which appeared in 1880, Peter Lavrov depicted the inability of the Communards to put an efficient army into the field against the forces of the Versailles Assembly in the following words:

"Neither the socialists nor the democratic extremists, both of whom were drawn from the ranks of the peaceful working classes and clerks, could provide military specialists. The usual occupations and general trend of thought of these leaders of a people's revolution made them strangers to military technique and unfitted them for the task of controlling the actions of military leaders. The government was incompetent to direct in affairs of war; consequently all military discipline was undermined, while the military leaders were deprived of the possibility of taking quick and energetic action at the very moment when the fate of the Commune depended on the speed and energy of their actions."

Lissagaray, who fought for the Commune, describes the state of the troops as follows:

"Most battalions had no leaders. The cadres of the National Guard were incomplete, while the generals who took the responsibility of leading 40,000 men had never taken even a single battalion into action. They neglected the most elementary arrangements; they failed to provide artillery, powder wagons and ambulances. One day they even forgot to issue any orders, and so left their men for hours without food in a cold, wet fog."

It was the experience of the Paris Commune that led Karl Kautsky to the opinion that "warfare is not the proletariat's strong point."

But meanwhile almost half a century had elapsed. The proletariat had learnt much since 1871, even in the military sphere. The Russian soldiers drawn from the classes of workers and peasants were able to make a practical study of warfare in the Russo-Japanese War of 1904 and the imperialist World War.

But the bourgeoisie also had learnt much. Military technique and tactics had undergone extensive developments, while we must also take into consideration the fact that the pre-revolutionary Russian Army was far behind other modern armies in those respects as well as in the important matters of military organization and administration. So long as the Russian Red forces had to fight only Russian White forces organized and led by Russian officers, the backward condition of the old Tsarist Army was actually an asset to the Soviet Army, because its own ranks contained many former prisoners-of-war, including soldiers, N.C.O.s, and even a few officers of the German and Austro–Hungarian armies. Moreover, less time and trouble were needed to bring individual soldiers and officers—or even whole army corps—up to the backward Tsarist standard, than to the higher standard of a modern army. But the backwardness of the old army was in itself the cause of the magnitude of the danger which an intervention threatened.

The creation of a body of qualified officers was a matter of life and death for the Soviet Republic. The Bolshevist Party had made no preparations to deal with such a problem. In March 1919, Lenin drew attention to the fact that "the former teachers of socialism who foresaw and prophesied so many events of the social revolution never discussed the question of utilizing the reserves of bourgeois knowledge and technique accumulated by the worst forms of militarism."

Lenin, indeed, had given keen attention to military problems in pre-revolutionary days. Clausewitz's profound work *On War* became his text-book of military knowledge, and he applied his instructor's system of thought to the problems raised in the art of armed insurrection and revolutionary warfare. During his period of exile in Switzerland in the early years of the World War he translated the memoirs of the Commune General Cluseret and published them with a preface of his own. But neither Cluseret nor the military-technical works of Friedrich Engels nor those of Bebel and Jaurès on the militia dealt with the basic problem of the creation of a Red Army or the employment of military specialists to raise and lead the armed forces of the Revolution.

The Proletarian Officer Cadres

In the first months following the October Revolution, and especially in the period immediately preceding Brest-Litovsk, the Red Guard officers were drawn almost exclusively from the Bolshevist military cadres and the N.C.O.s of the old army. These men also provided the nucleus of the officers of the regular Red Army.

The N.C.O.s of the old army were frequently elected as representatives in the Soldiers' Councils at the time of the February Revolution. They learnt to take command of large military formations and so provided the Soviet power with a core of leaders who remained loyal to it. But during the war years these N.C.O.s had been forced to limit their activities in the sphere of military organization and tactics to units ranging from a platoon to a company. The consequence was that they often had

a good eye for tactical work, but their capacity for turning armed hordes into military formations and for leading those formations was somewhat akin to the capacity
that might be expected from a backwoodsman. When
promoted to command armies, they still retained the
limited outlook of corporals.

The most important of the army commanders who
have risen from the ranks of the old Tsarist N.C.O.s are
the present Marshals Blücher, Voroshilov and Budyonny, to whom may be added the guerilla leader
Chapayev, who fell in 1919. Budyonny served in the
ranks in the Russo–Japanese War, and became a
sergeant-major in the World War.

Most of the Bolshevist military workers acquired the
knowledge and capability of army leaders in an amaz-
ingly short time, despite the fact that they had done no
previous military service. These 'civilians' had one
great advantage over the N.C.O.s, in that their outlook
was not restricted by the corporal's point of view and
they were well aware of their lack of military knowledge.
The non-commissioned officer who had served at the
front often imagined himself a master of all military
wisdom because he had shown himself superior to his
lieutenant or captain in the practical duties connected
with his company.

The military workers generally won their way to high
command by promotion from the ranks of the war
commissars or revolutionary councils of war. The most
successful army commanders from the ranks of the old

Bolshevist military workers are Antonov-Ovsenenko, Frunse, Trotsky's successor in the War Commissariat, Yakir, the Commander-in-Chief of the Ukraine Military District, who was shot alongside Tuchachevsky in May 1937, Georgi Piatakov, who served on the revolutionary councils of war of various armies and was shot in January 1937, Smirnov, who served on the revolutionary councils of war for the eastern and south-eastern fronts, the western front in the Polish War and the Caucasus front and died in one of Stalin's prisons, and Ivan Smilga, whom Lenin and Trotsky sent to preside over one revolutionary council of war after another, whenever the situation was critical at the front in question. His name is linked with many a great victory won by the Red Army, but he was shot in January 1937.

Naturally, the number of proletarian non-commissioned officers and old military workers was far too small to fill all the officers' posts in an army of 5,000,000 men. Moreover, they were not in a position to succeed in organizing, training and leading armies without expert assistance. As far back as the spring of 1918 military schools were established for the purpose of supplying further cadres of proletarian commanders, but even these were very far from filling the gaps. Trotsky has given us the following description of them:

"In the first period the military schools showed signs of the general weakness of our military organization. The short courses, lasting but a few months, could turn out only middling soldiers for a Red Army, but no leaders. Since, however, large masses of men were being sent to the front at that time, most of whom did not handle a rifle until they were entrained, these Red Army men who had undergone a four months' course were required not merely to take charge of squads; they had to command half-companies, and even companies."

But the military schools could not achieve even these feeble results without employing a considerable number of officers belonging to the old army.

The Officers of the Old Army.

The problem of the employment of military specialists in an army raised by the dictatorship of the proletariat is an old one. It is part of the problem arising from the relations of the revolutionary party to the middle classes in general and to bourgeois experts and scientists in particular.

The Russian officer class was never a well-knit, homogeneous body of men. Strong revolutionary traditions and tendencies had always existed in it side by side with the reactionary ones. In every great political and social struggle undertaken by the Russian people there were always officers in the revolutionary camp.

The leaders of the Decabrist Rebellion of 1827, which aimed at the overthrow of Tsarism and the establishment of a democratic republic, were officers. Officers also played leading parts in the great peasant insurrection in the second half of the previous century. In the 'seventies the celebrated Narodnik Shelyabov, who was of serf descent, contrived to rally to his cause a number of St. Petersburg officers, including several of high rank, who sided with the people in the fight against serfdom and Tsarism and ended their lives on the gallows for the sake of the Revolution. The traditions of the Russian officer class also keep immortal the name of Lieutenant Schmidt, who led the sailors of the Black Sea Fleet in their mutiny in 1905, and was ultimately court-martialled and shot.

In the first days of the October Revolution numerous officers (especially from the junior ranks) offered their services to the Soviet party. The best type of these progressive officers was represented by a certain M. N. Tuchachevsky, who came from an old aristocratic family that traced its descent from the Counts of Flanders. One of Tuchachevsky's ancestors was the son of a Count of Flanders who vanished after fighting in the Holy Land as a crusader. For a long time nothing was heard of him, until he made a sudden reappearance in the Odessa district, in company with a young Turkish wife. There he took service with a Russian prince, who gave him the tenure of the village of Tuchachev.

Young Tuchachevsky grew up steeped in the ideas of the French Revolution and of the Decabrists and Narodniki. Passing out of the Military School in 1914, he was sent to the front as a sub-lieutenant when the World War broke out. In 1915 he was taken prisoner by the Germans.

On the triumph of the February Revolution, he made one attempt after another to escape. He did not succeed in getting away until his fifth effort, when he broke out of the fortress of Ingolstadt, in Bavaria. On the eve of this escape he said to a French fellow-prisoner: "In a year I shall be either a general or a corpse."

The young popular lieutenant of the Guards was elected company-leader by his men shortly after his arrival in Petrograd. Then he reported to Sklansky, who was Trotsky's representative at the time. Trotsky, recognizing the great military talents and upright character of the young officer, appointed him to a post in the Military Section of the Central Executive Committee of the Soviets. Later we find Tuchachevsky entrusted with the organization and supreme command of the First Red Army when the Czechoslovak Legion rose against the Soviets in May 1918.

Thousands of junior officers entered the Red Army along with Tuchachevsky; it was not long before some of them were commanding divisions, corps and armies. In addition to Tuchachevsky, we may mention the following who won distinction :

Uborevitch, who commanded the 14th, 11th and 13th Red Armies in the campaigns against Denikin and Wrangel in 1919 and 1920, and was in supreme command of the revolutionary armies of the Far East in

1921-2, when he completed the liberation of that area from the White Guards and Japanese by the occupation of Vladivostok. He was shot in May 1937.

Primakov, who after Budyonny, was the best cavalry commander of the Civil War, and led a Red cavalry division on almost every front. At the end of the Civil War he was put in charge of the Kremlin Commander School; later on he acted as deputy Commander-in-Chief of the Ukraine military district. He, too, was shot in May 1937.

Putna, a mighty hero of the Civil War, who commanded a division in the Polish campaign and was shot alongside his former chief, Tuchachevsky, in May 1937.

One of the first general staff officers to offer his services to the Red Army was the Tsarist officer, Colonel S. Kamenev, who came of an old military family. After serving with distinction in a number of high positions, he was appointed Commander-in-Chief of all the armed forces of the Republic on June 1, 1919. When the Civil War ended, he became inspector of the staff of the Red Army, then chief of the staff, and in May 1927, vice-president of the Revolutionary Council of War, which post he held until he was superseded by Tuchachevsky.

Among the other staff officers, most of whom were originally *Polkovniki* (colonels commanding regiments) we may mention Vazetis, who was the first Commander-in-Chief of the armed forces of the Republic, but

became an instructor at the General Staff War Academy
in 1919; Kork, a former student at the Tsarist War
Academy, who commanded an army during the Civil
War and afterwards became director of the War
Academy, and was shot in May 1937; Yegerov, Tucha-
chevsky's successor, who commanded an army on the
southern front with distinction during the Civil War;
Shaposhnikov, who did not enter the Red Army until
some time later, and held no command in the Civil
War, during which he was employed on staff work at
the base. Since the execution of Tuchachevsky and
other Red Army leaders, Shaposhnikov, Yegerov and
Voroshilov have been the principal chiefs of the Red
Army.

Patriotic feelings were the main motives which
induced a number of officers of the old army to offer
their services in good faith to the Soviet Government,
to which they had been originally hostile. They came to
realize that Russia's national freedom was indissolubly
linked with the Soviet Power, and saw that all 'patriotic
associations' fighting against the Soviets were forced to
become the agents of imperialist powers striving to lay
hands on the cornfields and oil and mineral deposits in
'Russian soil.'

In his work entitled *Trotsky and the Red Army*,
published in 1923, Karl Radek describes his experiences
with a military expert who accompanied the Russian
delegation to the Brest-Litovsk conference. At first
his attitude and that of his brother officers towards the

delegates led by Trotsky was something more than
frigid. They thought they had been dragged there as
unwilling participants in a pre-arranged comedy, for
they considered the Bolshevists as agents of German
imperialism. But, Radek tells us, "As soon as Trotsky
began to oppose the demands of German imperialism
on behalf of the principles of the Russian Revolution,
the initial mistrust of the Russian military experts
dwindled daily. I can still remember the night when
Admiral Altvater came into my room and said in all
sincerity: 'I came here because I was forced to. I didn't
trust you. But now I shall help you and do my duty as
never before, for I sincerely believe I shall be serving my
country in so doing.' "

When Pilsudski marched his forces into Russian
territory in 1920 without any declaration of war, and
occupied a part of the Ukraine, a white-bearded cripple
came to the gates of the Kremlin and insisted on seeing
Kalinin, Trotsky, or some other member of the government. At first he refused to give his name to the
sentinel, merely stating that he was a former army
officer who desired to offer his services to the Red
Army.

He was Brussilov, formerly Commander-in-Chief of
the Tsarist Army. While living in concealment in a
private house in Moscow during the Civil War, he was
severely wounded by shell-fire and lost a leg in consequence. This saved his life, for otherwise he would
probably have been shot by the Red Guards, who held

him responsible for the butcheries of the imperialist
war.

For a long time he had lived in complete seclusion,
but now his patriotism drove him into the arms of the
Soviet Government. He brought with him a copy of a
proclamation calling upon all former officers to join the
Red Army and help to deliver their country from the
foreign invaders.

Trotsky appointed Brussilov president of the Special
Council of War attached to the Commander-in-Chief
of the Red Army. Subsequently this veteran served as
inspector of cavalry from 1922 to 1924 when he retired.
In 1925 he died, and was given a State funeral, his body
being borne to the cemetery on a gun-carriage. When
the three volleys had been fired, the priests took charge
of it and buried it in a monastery with the rites of the
Orthodox Church.

General Nikolayev, an officer of the old Tsarist
Army, was taken prisoner in 1919 by General Yudenitch
in the vicinity of Petrograd when leading troops of the
Red Army. At first Yudenitch desired to take him into
his service; he sent for him and offered him his hand.
But Nikolayev refused to shake hands with 'an execu-
tioner of the Russian people and an agent of the interventionists.' Therefore Yudenitch condemned him to
be hanged, and Nikolayev called out when the rope was
round his neck: "Long live the Red Army! I declare
that I have served the workmen and peasants to my last
breath!"

The greater number of former officers were incorporated in the Red Army by means of a compulsory mobilization. In 1924 one of these men, who was then commanding a division in the Red Army, told me the story of his career.

He was already a colonel in the Russian Army when he served as a volunteer with the French in the Great War. In 1916 he commanded a Moroccan division at Verdun. He won the Cross of the Legion of Honour and numerous other distinctions which were awarded him for his valour. When hostilities ceased between Germany and Russia, he returned home and lived very quietly in Samara. He was arrested in the winter of 1918–9.

Every day men of the Red Army took prisoners out of the mass cells and shot them. One day his name was read out at the morning roll-call, and he was conveyed along with some twenty other former officers to a waiting lorry, which drove off out of the town. The prisoners were convinced they were going to be shot, but the lorry drew up at a building, where armed men escorted them into a room. Thence they were taken one by one into an adjoining room, from which they did not return.

At last my friend's turn came. In the adjoining room he was received by a Red commissar, by whose side stood a workman, clad in a leather jacket, with a rifle slung over his shoulder and a revolver in his belt. The commissar handed him a document which proved to be a copy of Trotsky's decree for the mobilization of former officers. The colonel signed a sworn declaration to the effect that he would serve the Soviet Union and the Red Army faithfully. He was then informed that his wife and family would be held responsible for any treachery he might commit.

Three minutes later the Tsarist colonel sat in a car as commander of a regiment of Red riflemen. Beside him sat the regimental commissar, who turned out to be the workman in the leather jacket. On their way to the front the latter described the state of affairs in his regiment; there was no proper leadership and no discipline; there were not sufficient rifles to go round. The Red soldiers were strongly suspicious of all former Tsarist officers, while the new commander might expect obstinate resistance from the former non-commissioned officers, who had hitherto occupied all posts of command in the regiment.

The colonel reached his regiment that same night. Two days later it went into action. The colonel, who so far had kept himself in the background, seized a rifle and stormed the enemy positions at the head of his men.

That was the end of the opposition to the Tsarist officer. After the battle the soldiers carried their 'red commander' on their shoulders to the market-place, where they held a meeting in his honour. This former Tsarist colonel was promoted for his valour to the command of a division, and later on commanded an army corps and received two 'Orders of the Red Flag.'

Many Tsarist officers, including some who volunteered for service with the Red Army, were guilty of treachery. At an assembly of 3,000 military specialists in Petrograd in October 1919, Zinoviev described a typical case:

"I made Neklyudov's acquaintance when he was the Red officer in command of Krasnaya Gorka. He was then a young man of a good old family which had produced many liberals in the reigns of Alexander II and Alexander III. He helped to build this fortress, and I should have imagined every stone of Krasnaya Gorka was dear to him. In Tsarist days he was a fifth wheel to the wagon, because the old bureaucrats were not minded to let the descendant of liberal ancestors receive advancement. Under the Soviet Government he was put in charge of Krasnaya Gorka. There he had a chance to apply his talents; he received every possible aid he needed to develop them. How then could we anticipate treachery from such a man? But do you know what he did? He handed over Krasnaya Gorka to the Finnish White Guards."

Colonel M. A. Muraviov was another traitor. From him, too, anything but treachery was anticipated. During the October Revolution he was in command of the Red forces which the Revolutionary War Committee sent against General Krasnov, who was advancing on Petrograd. Afterwards he had a command on the Rumanian front, while later he was appointed

Commander-in-Chief of the Red troops in the Ukraine.
In the summer of 1918 the Soviet Government appointed
him Commander-in-Chief of the forces in the Volga and
Ural districts.

This was at the time of the Czechoslovak revolt
against the Soviet authorities. The most important
basis of operations for the Red forces was Lenin's native
town, Simbirsk. Muraviov entered this town with a
detachment of troops, who were devoted to him
personally and officered by Left Social Revolutionaries;
there he invited the leading Bolshevists to meet him,
arrested them, and made arrangements to seize the
person of Tuchachevsky, who was then in command of
the 1st Red Army. But the latter, who was protected by
his own men, organized the resistance to this treachery.

Muraviov issued a proclamation: "Peace with the
Czechs, who are our Slav brothers! War with Germany!
It was not long before he was arrested and shot, but for
a time his treachery caused such disorganization in the
army that Simbirsk fell into the hands of the Czechs
and Whites.

Many officers committed acts of treachery because
their bourgeois class-consciousness was stronger than
their patriotic feelings. They often deserted to the
imperialist forces, but the Bolshevists assessed such
treachery as one of the inevitable "unproductive
expenses" incurred by the proletariat in its work of
building up its class army.

The Political Commissars.

The Soviet authorities endeavoured to reduce these 'unproductive expenses' to a minimum by means of the political commissars who were attached to the old officers. First and foremost they endeavoured to dissipate the natural mistrust felt by the Red soldiers towards the employment of military specialists by enacting that every Tsarist officer should be accompanied by a commissar, who had to countersign every order given by the commanding officer before it became effective. The commissar was, in fact, the Soviet Government's direct representative with the army.

The command of fronts and armies was entrusted to "Revolutionary Councils of War," consisting of one commanding officer and one or two commissars. There were commissars for every corps and division, while others were attached to the smaller units down to battalions and sometimes even to companies.

The functions of the Revolutionary Councils of War and the commissars were essentially the same, though within differing frameworks. The commissars were not allowed to interfere with the work of leadership or with tactical measures, and in all matters of actual operations they were compelled to countersign even those orders of which they did not approve; in such cases, however, they had a right of protest to a higher authority. In all other spheres of activity the commissar had a voice equal to that of the commanding officer.

Naturally there was often friction between the two since it was impossible to draw a definite line between their powers. Only too frequently this kind of friction crippled for a time the activities of large bodies of troops. The army order issued by Trotsky on August 5, 1918, at a period when the commissar's office was just beginning to become a regular piece of army mechanism, is characteristic of the way in which he dealt with such difficulties. It runs as follows:

"Re the participation of officers in White Guard revolts, I note that quarrels between commissars and military leaders have lately been increasing. From the evidence at my disposal it is apparent that commissars often take a directly wrong line of action, either by usurping operative and leadership functions, or by poisoning the relations between officer and commissar by a policy of petty quibbling carried out in a spirit of undignified rivalry. At the same time it not infrequently happens that the presence of the commissar does not prevent the military commander from deserting to the enemy.

"In view of these circumstances I must bring the following facts to the notice of all commissars:

"(1) A commissar is not there to give orders, but to watch. He must watch carefully and sharply.

"(2) A commissar must behave respectfully to military experts who fulfil their duties conscientiously, and must protect their rights and human dignities by all the means of the Soviet authority.

"(3) A commissar must not seek quarrels, but if he finds it necessary to intervene, his intervention must be effective.

"(4) Offences against this order will be subject to severe penalties.

"(5) A commissar who fails to prevent the desertion of a commanding officer will have to answer for his negligence with his own life."

On the whole the commissars justified themselves as necessary accessories to the employment of former Tsarist officers in the organization and command of the Red Army. "Only the happy combination of a communist and a general staff officer will ensure 100 per cent efficiency in the leadership," wrote the former Tsarist general staff officer and Red Army commander, S. Kamenev in an army order he issued in 1920.

The office of commissar was conceived as a temporary measure which the creation of a reliable corps of Soviet officers would gradually render unnecessary.

Statistics.

We can estimate the magnitude of the problem presented by the employment of Tsarist officers in the Red Army and successfully solved by Lenin and Trotsky only by studying the statistics concerning the officers who served in this army during the Civil War.

When the old Tsarist Army collapsed, it left a legacy of about 500,000 officers of all ranks. At first sight these figures may appear too large, especially if compared with the present figures in time of peace, and if we forget to take into account the vast dimensions to which the Tsarist Army swelled in the World War.

In 1917 the number of men serving in the Tsarist forces reached a total of 12,000,000—for we must deduct 7,000,000 casualties from the 19,000,000 mobilized. Including all the officers in the general staff and military administration, we thus arrive at a proportion of one officer to every twenty-four men in the old Tsarist Army.

According to the material supplied by Captain Peter Wright in his work, *At the Supreme War Council*, the total British Army in March 1918, including coloured troops but excluding the labour battalions, consisted of 220,770 officers and 4,761,484 men, so that we find one officer to only twenty-one men.

According to the statistics of the Russian General Staff, about 200,000 of the 500,000 officers of the

Tsarist Army served on the side of the Whites or in the interventionist armies during the Civil War. We may estimate the number serving in the Red Army as about 100,000, including the *Praportshiki* (ensigns). The number of officers serving in the fighting and administrative branches of the Red Army on January 1, 1919, totalled 165,113 persons of all ranks who had served in the old army, according to the statistics of the general staff.

On August 15, 1920, the Red Army contained :

214,717 *Praportshiki* and N.C.O.s.
48,409 Officers of the rank of lieutenant and upwards
10,339 Military Officials
13,949 Doctors and Veterinary Surgeons
26,766 Other Ambulance Personnel

Total 314,180 military specialists of the old army

By the end of December 1920, the Red military schools had provided 39,914 junior officers for the army, which then possessed a total of 130,000 officers and 315,747 N.C.O.s and military officials.

In view of this mass employment of former Tsarist officers in the Red Army, the question naturally arises why it was necessary to demolish the edifice of the old army completely, leaving not one stone upon another, so to speak, and then to use these same stones for the laborious erection of a new building. Why was it necessary to apply the Bolshevist recipe for the disintegration of the army instead of reforming it by means of a democratic permeation?

The answer is that the acquisition of a quarter of the total Tsarist officer effectives for an army of a socialist type was a political and not a mathematical task. It was necessary for the Revolution to possess sufficient power to carry some of these officers over to its side and extract compulsory service from others before it could draft them all into a revolutionary army and make sure that in it they would serve the cause of the proletariat instead of putting the proletariat into uniform to serve the interests of the exploiting classes.

When Mechonoshin, a member of the first College of War Commissars, paid a visit to the Ministry of War shortly after the October Revolution, he was received by General Babikov in military style. All his questions and objections were met with a laconic military "Yes." Mechonoshin left the War Office with the certain conviction that "this machine cannot be remodelled. It is more likely to change us than be changed by us. It is the system that we shall have to demolish. We must carefully preserve and lay aside all that is valuable in it, so that we can use it when building up the new machine and our new military organization."

The generalization and amplification given by Lenin to this empirical judgement passed by a Bolshevist working man of Mechonoshin's type must serve as a guide to the line of action to be taken by the socialist proletariat: "We can only maintain ourselves in power by appropriating all the cultural and technical experience acquired by progressive capitalism and enlisting all its representatives in our service. Our Red Army won victories of a military nature only because we contrived to solve this problem."

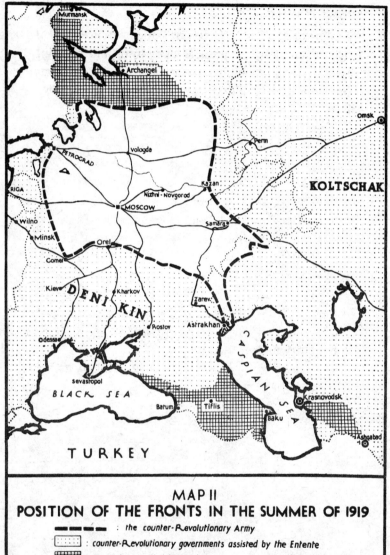

MAP II
POSITION OF THE FRONTS IN THE SUMMER OF 1919

- - - - : the counter-Revolutionary Army

. . . . : counter-Revolutionary governments assisted by the Entente

▦ : territories occupied by English troops   ⊙ : English garrisons

Chapter Three

Historical Analogies.

The armed conflict against internal counter-revolution began even before the seizure of power by the Bolshevists. When, in August 1917, General Kornilov marched on Petrograd, his main blow was aimed at the rising socialist proletariat rather than the vacillating bourgeois democracy. But the hard struggle for self-preservation and the consolidation and amplification of the October Revolution, which lasted nearly four years, did not begin until after the easily won victory of that October of 1917.

The Civil War, which tortured the land to its very marrow and claimed untold victims, was not a phenomenon peculiar to the Russian Revolution. "History shows no instance of a revolution which may be considered an accomplished fact when it has proved successful, or which will allow the rebels to rest on their laurels when it is over." In these words Lenin did no more than utter a historical truth which is as old as classes and class wars.

There is always something fascinating about historical

---

[1] See also Appendix II: *Chronicle of The Civil War.*

analogies between revolutions. Comparisons between
the October Revolution and the French Revolution are
frequently drawn; the revolutionary wars each country
was forced to wage after overthrowing the old régime,
and their onset and ending, are reduced all too readily
to a common denominator. But we must "use such
analogies with the greatest caution," as Trotsky rightly
pointed out in his *Military Doctrine* (1921), "for otherwise," he continues, "the superficial resemblances may
induce us to forget the material differences." Trotsky's
criticism is all the more instructive since he has failed
to follow his own advice in that he is now led to draw
an unwary comparison between Stalinism and Bonapartism on the ground of superficial resemblances.
Therein he overlooks the fact that the material and
social-economic causes of Bonapartism were to be
found in the destruction of small-scale production,
whereas Stalinism has risen to power on an economic
basis of State monopolies.

In the work already quoted, Trotsky writes: "When
discussing revolutionary wars, we are most frequently
influenced by memories of the wars of the French
Revolution. Therein we forget that at the end of the
eighteenth century France was the richest and most
civilized country of the European continent, whereas
twentieth-century Russia was the poorest and most
backward European land. The revolutionary task of
the French Army was far more superficial in character
than the revolutionary tasks before us now. In those

days the main objective was the overthrow of the
'tyrants' and the abolition or modification of feudal
serfdom. Our mission, on the other hand, is the
complete destruction of exploitation and class oppression."

The absolute and relative poverty and backwardness
of Russia combined with the material and social-
political substance of the proletarian revolution to
stamp their own particular impress on the Russian Civil
War. The great majority of the Russian population
belonged to the lower middle classes, while according
to the last pre-War statistics 86.5 of this population
lived on the land, against only 13.5 in the towns.

"Russia is so large and so variegated," wrote Lenin
in a polemic against the 'left' communists in May 1918,
"that the most varying types of social and economic
conditions are intertwined one with another. We have
(1) the patriarchal peasant economic system, which to
a very large extent is natural economy; (2) the economic
system of the petty trader (which includes the majority
of the peasants who sell bread); (3) the private economic
system of capitalism; (4) State capitalism; (5) socialism
(since the victory of the October Revolution). The
main social-economic war will develop into a struggle
of the lower middle classes plus private capitalism,
against State capitalism and socialism."

A survey of this social-economic structure of Russia
reveals the futility of historical comparisons between
the objectives, tendencies of development and degenera-

tive manifestations (Thermidor!) of the French Revolution and the October Revolution.

From the Peace of Brest-Litovsk to the Entente's Intervention.

After the victories of the Revolution in Petrograd and Moscow the authority of the Soviet Government overflowed the whole vast realm like a mighty stream that carries everything with it. The Soviets in the towns and on the land came under Bolshevist leadership, the old officials were hunted out of office, the workers took possession of the factories, and the peasants seized the estates of the Crown, the Church, and the landed proprietors. When manifestations of resistance appeared locally, they were dealt with by small shock troops of Red Guards or detachments of pro-revolution soldiers sent from the capital or acting on their own initiative. This elemental force of the first revolutionary wave caused a panic in the camp of the counter-revolutionists, and a temporary paralysis of all forces hostile to the Revolution.

The only opposition that still held out was the *Rada* of the Ukraine, which was more or less akin to the Kerensky Government in its political aspect, but possessed strong separatist Ukrainian-nationalistic features. Even after the victory of the proletarian revolution, the centuries of oppression by the Great Russians proved an obstacle to an independent class movement in the ranks of the proletariat of the races formerly oppressed.

The *Rada* still held sway in Kiev, the old Ukrainian capital situated in the midst of the plains, but a Central Executive Committee of the Soviets had been formed at Kharkov, the centre of the Ukrainian industrial and mining area, and was gradually extending its power westward. Both these bodies sent peace delegations to Brest-Litovsk, but during the negotiations Soviet troops occupied Kiev on February 8, 1918, and the *Rada* government fled to Zhitomir. The representatives of German and Austro-Hungarian imperialism then concluded a treaty with this landless government, which, as Trotsky remarked, had "no territory for its basis except the citadel of Brest-Litovsk." They thought by this step to put pressure on the Russian Soviet delegation; moreover, there were reasons of home politics which made them anxious to give their peoples a 'peace' as a stimulant to further "prosecution of the war to a final victory."

For the moment this German manœuvre could do nothing to influence the fate of the *Rada*. The Ukraine was occupied by Red troops led by Antonov-Ovseyenko and Georgi Piatakov, the latter becoming head of the first Ukrainian Soviet Government, which was then formed.

The Rumanians occupied Bessarabia during the Brest-Litovsk negotiations. In February they were heavily defeated by Red Guard troops led by Colonel

Muraviov, who was destined later to turn traitor when
fighting against the Czechoslovaks. In this campaign
Chinese labour corps fighting on the Soviet side won
distinction; they were organized and led by a twenty-
one-year-old Jewish student from Kishinev named
Yakir, while another successful leader of Red forces on
the Bessarabian front was Uborevitch, who had become
a member of the Bolshevist Party in 1917.

Under pressure of their defeat the Rumanians made
a peace offer which envisaged the complete evacuation
of Bessarabia. Peace was concluded on this basis on
March 8, 1918. Then the Germans occupied the
Ukraine, and, feeling secure under the protection of
Wilhelm's bayonets, the Rumanians remained in
Bessarabia. Uborevitch threw his troops against the
advancing Germans, but after fierce fighting they were
dispersed. He was wounded and taken prisoner, but
managed to escape before he had fully recovered from
his injuries.

Meanwhile the Red Guards suppressed two revolts
organized by counter-revolutionary officers.

A large number of officers had left the army some time
before its break-up. They gathered together in the Don
area, which was mainly agricultural, and at Orenburg
in the Urals. The latter district provided a very favourable basis of operations for a counter-revolution, because the majority of the workers were small owners
and landed proprietors, while the mixture of many
nationalities was another asset. The most important

non-Russian racial group was that of the Bashkirs, who
had been involved in conflicts with the Russians on the
question of land ownership from time immemorial.
The White generals were able to exploit these racial
antagonisms for their own purposes.

In the Orenburg steppes the Cossack Hetman Dutov
raised White volunteer formations composed of officers
of the old army and Ural Cossacks. But he was defeated
by local Red Guard forces, led by the Bolshevist metal-
worker Medvedyev, who won the nickname of 'Marshal
Forward' by the celerity of his military operations and
from the slogan 'Forward' which he always wrote in
his daily orders and invariably uttered when he led the
Red Guards personally into action. He is known to-day
as Marshal Blücher, and we may add that in 1918 he was
the first to be decorated with the Order of the Red Flag.

The concentration of White Guard officer formations
under Generals Kornilov and Kaledin in the Don area
was a far greater menace to the new Soviet Government.
Since the *Rada* Government was not yet expelled from
the Ukraine, Kaledin was in a position to cut Russia off
from her richest coalfields by a successful advance, as
well as from her European granary if he managed to
effect a junction with the *Rada*. Moreover, Kaledin had
ample man-power at his disposal for recruiting purposes
in the Cossacks of the Don steppes; but, on the other
hand, the social structure of these Cossacks was by no
means a homogeneous one. Of their 2,000,000 population 1,800,000 were peasants, including 500,000 landless

peasants. Therein, and in the great proletarian oasis of
the steppes known as the Don basin, lay the great weakness of the Whites in the Don area.

The main Red plan of operations aimed at driving a
wedge between the Ukraine and the Don and thrusting
forward as far as Rostov on the Sea of Azov in order to
annihilate each set of opponents separately. Under the
leadership of Antonov-Ovseyenko this task was fulfilled in the shortest possible time.

Three Red Guard detachments, led by Sivers, Sablin
and Petrov, converged on Rostov, which was occupied
on March 8, 1918. Kaledin had committed suicide a
month previously, when he lost faith in his power to win
the Don Cossacks over to his counter-revolution.
General Kornilov, who after his death assumed the
supreme command, managed to escape after the capture
of Rostov and the dispersal of the White Guard volunteers.

The Reds who defeated the officers' volunteer formations were a strangely improvised force, in which
worker detachments of Red Guards fought in tactical
co-operation with formations composed of the remnants
of old regulars. The main fighting took place along the
line of the railway, where the Reds were forced to
advance in three successive groups in order to co-
ordinate the varying reliability of their different units.
In the van was an armoured train, behind which followed
the Red Guards, while the formations from the remnants
of the old army brought up the rear.

The suppression of both these officers' revolts proved that the counter-revolutionaries were not in a position to overthrow the power of the Soviet by means of internal force alone. Henceforth they made every endeavour to obtain armed assistance from abroad; that is, the Russian counter-revolutionaries became 'native auxiliaries' of the imperialist powers. Their patriotism was thereby shown up as treason against national interests in favour of foreign imperialism. The words of Karl Marx, written in 1871 in his *Civil War in France*, came true; as he then said: "Class rule is no longer in a position to disguise itself in a national uniform; all nationalist governments are united against the proletariat."

After the expulsion of the *Rada* from Kiev and the crushing of Dutov and Kaledin, the middle of February 1918 saw almost the whole of Russia in the hands of the Soviets. But the following weeks were to reveal the instability of the political basis on which the dictatorship of the proletariat rested.

In the second half of February the forces of German imperialism occupied the Baltic States and suppressed the Revolution there with much bloodshed. At the same time they began to advance into the Ukraine for reasons which we find enumerated in the diary of General Hoffmann, who wrote on February 17, 1918: "To-morrow we are going to begin hostilities against the Bolshevists. There is no other alternative, for otherwise these fellows will kill off the Ukrainians, Finns and

Balts, raise a new revolutionary army at their leisure, and do their dirty work all over Europe."

In pursuance of this 'European mission' of German imperialism Kiev was occupied; two weeks later it was the turn of Odessa; in April the Germans were in Kharkov. The chiefs of the Red Army could despatch only 15,000 fighting men against the enemy's twenty-nine infantry divisions, and four and a half cavalry divisions, which constitute an army of 200–250,000 men.

The Germans set up the Tsarist General Skoropadski as Hetman; with the help of German bayonets he established a bloody military dictatorship. The Red Guards evacuated the Ukraine almost without a fight, but an illegal Bolshevist revolutionary committee remained behind in Kiev, where it functioned under the leadership of Georgi Piatakov, whose elder brother Leonid had directed the illegal Bolshevist military work in January 1918, during the régime of the *Rada*, until he was arrested and murdered after bestial tortures. But Georgi Piatakov was destined to be shot by Stalin nineteen years later.

Among the members of this illegal revolutionary committee were Skripnik, Satonsky, Aussem and Bubnov. (Skripnik was People's Commissar for the Ukraine in 1937, when he committed suicide just before his arrest.) The functions of this committee comprised disorganization of the enemy's lines of communication, revolutionary propaganda among the armies of occupation, and preparation for revolts.

The German troops occupied the Ukraine and the whole southern portion of European Russia, advancing as far as the coasts of the Sea of Azov.

The Beginning of the Entente's Intervention.

The end of May 1918, saw the beginning of an adventure that took place along a 3,000-kilometre stretch of the Trans-Siberian Railway. Its scope extended from Irkutsk on Lake Baikal to Samara on the Volga, and it provided the sparks that were to set alight the internal counter-revolution.

During the World War there had come into existence in Russia a Czechoslovak Legion, composed mainly of Austrian prisoners of war of Czech nationality. This body of men was in the Ukraine at the time of the October Revolution, and promptly declared its neutrality.[1]

The Czechs retreated to Soviet Russian soil when the Germans occupied the Ukraine. It was agreed with the Soviet Government that they should be entrained on the Trans-Siberian Railway and sent to Vladivostok, where they could take ship for France. But the occupation of this port by the Japanese induced the Soviet authorities to change their plans, for they feared that a junction of armed Czech forces with the Japanese might lead to a strengthening of the anti-Soviet front in Siberia. They

[1] Jaroslav Hashek, who was later destined to win universal fame with his cultural-historical war novel *The Good Soldier Schweik*, fought in their ranks.

therefore opened fresh negotiations with the Czechs and French, with a view to arranging for the Legion to march to Archangelsk. Then, at the end of May 1918 the Czechoslovak Legion rose up in insurrection against the Soviet authorities.

Soviet rule collapsed along the whole length of the Trans-Siberian Railway, in the vast area of the European Volga basin and as far as the heart of Siberia. The Czechoslovaks occupied almost simultaneously Samara on the Volga, Chelyanbinsk in the Urals and Novo-Nikolayevsk (now known as Novo-Sibirsk) when marching on the Trans-Siberian Railway in three columns. Their numbers were not great, amounting only to some 40,000 men in all, so that the weakness of the Soviet Government and the fickleness of the Russian peasantry and lower middle classes are amply demonstrated by the fact that forces so numerically feeble were able to take control of a region extending from the Volga to the Ob and thence to Lake Baikal, with a stretch of 3,000 kilometres of railway for their strategical basis.

General Stefanik, destined later to be the first Minister for War in the Czechoslovak Republic, supplied the international background for the Legion's action in a speech he made to the Czech soldiers during his sojourn in Siberia. "I can assure you," he said, "that the Entente will take responsibility for the fighting in which our Czechoslovak soldiers are now engaged, and that even the French Socialists have voted the money for the upkeep of the Czechoslovak troops in Siberia. This time I can guarantee that the Entente's action will take concrete form. As far as my information goes, the Allies themselves are about to begin hostilities against the Soviet forces, and will operate mainly in southern Russia, which General Berthelot is going to occupy with five divisions drawn from the Salonika and Rumanian fronts. At the same time the Entente troops in Murmansk will be reinforced."

Dr. Benes, the former Foreign Minister and present President of the Czechoslovak Republic, expresses similar views in his *Memoirs*, in which he says: "The problem of our Legion became an important element in the Allied policy and plan of campaign."

The 'Government of Siberia,' which was established at Omsk, and the 'Government of the Constituents' at Samara came into existence on the strength of the Czechoslovak insurrection. Both these governments were of a petty-bourgeois democratic nature.

Another Civil War front was formed at the same time in southern Russia. When the Germans advanced into the Don area which the Red Guards had cleared of Kaledin's White formations, the Cossacks rose up against the Soviets. A White Don Army was formed under the General Krasnov who was arrested after his attempt to suppress the rising in Petrograd in October 1917, and subsequently released on giving his word of honour to undertake no further action against the Soviets. The Kuban area, which comprised the rich

corn-growing steppes north of the Caucasus, where so
many Cossacks lived, was also lost to the Soviets, the
leader of the White Guard revolt there being General
Denikin.

The Russian bourgeoisie had recovered from its
panic. It soon abandoned defensive action and everywhere took the offensive. The Red Guards were unable
to cope with the regular military forces of the Whites.
They retreated almost without a fight. When they went
into action, they were defeated after a brief resistance.
The plight of the Red forces is depicted as follows by
Putna in his work on the Civil War:

"When Kazan yielded on August 6, 1918, to the
combined blows of the Czechs and White Russians, our
weak forces fled after their dispersal in a north-westerly
direction. They fled as men flee after a decisive—so it
then seemed—defeat which can never be counter-
balanced."

The deadly peril threatening the Soviet Republic
caused the views of Lenin and Trotsky in favour of a
centralized army assisted by military specialists to
prevail over the adherents of guerilla warfare. In fact
the Czechoslovak Legion was in some measure, though
unintentionally, the cause of the birth of the Red Army.
The Soviet Government proceeded to a mass mobilization; the men called up were equipped, armed, drafted
into formations and trained in the railway-trains and
on the march. The Revolutionary Council of War gave
orders for a temporary evacuation of the Tsaritsyn

sector on the southern front, since General Krasnov, who was still in process of organizing his White armies, threatened no immediate danger. K. Voroshilov, who was in command on that sector, refused to execute this order, and was supported in his insubordination by Stalin, who was attached to the southern army as a member of the local Revolutionary Council of War. The subsequent failure of the southern army on the battlefield of Simbirsk prevented the complete defeat of the Whites; according to a statement made by Tuchachevsky in 1922 in his capacity of director of the War Academy, this caused the Civil War to be prolonged by two years.

The confidence of the Russian proletariat in its ability to put up a successful resistance against the attacks of regular White formations was badly shaken. Matters were made worse by the treachery of Colonel Muraviov, which fell like a thunderbolt on a Red front in process of formation.

It was then that Trotsky took personal charge of operations at Sviyazhsk, near Kazan. On September 10, 1918, Putna took this town, and on September 12 the 1st Red Army, commanded by Tuchachevsky, won a decisive victory over the allied Czechoslovak and White Russian forces, recovered Simbirsk, and began the series of quick operations that freed the middle Volga area from the Whites.

The battle of Simbirsk was the first great victory won by the regular Red Army, Trotsky wrote as follows:

"That day was a noteworthy date in the history of the Red Army. At once we felt firm ground under our feet. The time of our first helpless efforts was over; thenceforth we were able to fight and win."

The Climax of the Civil War.

But the situation of the Soviet Republic still remained critical after the battle of Simbirsk. The Entente had landed English and American troops in Murmansk and Archangelsk in July and August. The Far East was occupied; an Allied army was formed under the command of a Japanese general, with whom the English General Knox was associated. It was made up of two Japanese divisions, 7,000 Americans, two English battalions and 3,000 French and Italians.

According to the statistics of the Russian General Staff, the interventionist forces in February 1919 reached a total of 300,000 men. Of these, 50,000 men composed the northern army, while Franco-Greek troops to the number of 20,000 along with 7,000 Americans, occupied the Black Sea coast. There were 40,000 men in the Finnish sector and another 37,000 in Estonia and Latvia. The Polish forces numbered 64,000 and the Czechoslovaks 40,000. The Japanese sent three divisions, and finally there were the 31,000 German Balts. These figures do not include the sailors of the British and French Fleets in the Baltic and Black Seas.

The Civil War ravaged Russia for three years, during

which victory fluctuated from one side to the other. It often looked as if the Soviet Republic was bound to be broken within a few weeks; there were also moments when hopes took the concrete form of a proletarian revolution hastening westwards in quick, bold leaps. Twice Bolshevism knocked at the gates of Central Europe—in the spring of 1919 and in the Polish campaign of 1920.

When the German armies of occupation that were disintegrating under Bolshevist influence streamed homewards after the triumph of the November Revolution in Germany and Austro-Hungary, the Red Army began to prepare itself for its mission of carrying the banner of the international proletarian revolution into the lands of the West. Those were the days when Lenin wrote:

"The Russian proletariat will understand that the time is close at hand when it must make its greatest sacrifices on behalf of internationalism. The day is approaching when circumstances will require us to give assistance against Anglo-French imperialism, to the German nation that has freed itself from its own imperialism. Therefore, let us begin our preparations without delay. Let us show that the workers of Russia can work all the more energetically, fight with greater self-sacrifice, and give their lives more readily when a revolution is at stake that is not merely a Russian affair but an affair of the international workers of the world."

In the spring of 1919 direct military intervention by

the Red Army in the international arena of the class war appeared to be only a matter of days. In Hungary and Bavaria the workers had seized power; the Hungarian Red Army was engaged on a victorious offensive. After reconquering the Ukraine, the Russian Red Army advanced in the direction of Carpathian Russia, where whole districts came under the control of Soviet guerilla forces. Every hour decreased the distance separating the Russian revolutionary forces advancing westward and those of the Hungarian pressing forward in a north-easterly direction.

Then the attack launched by Horthy's White Guards and their allied forces compelled the Hungarian Reds to suspend their advance in the north-east and throw all their forces on to their south-western front. At the same time the Russian Red Army troops marching towards Carpathian Russia had to be hastily transferred to the new eastern front that came into existence on the Volga and the southern front in the Ukraine and Don areas. Admiral Kolchak had succeeded in overthrowing the petty-bourgeois democratic 'Government of Siberia,' and his armies were approaching the Volga, while General Denikin, who had assumed the supreme command of all White Guard formations in southern Russia, was advancing against central Russia from his base at Kuban.

Denikin occupied the Don area and eastern Ukraine; his troops pressed forward to Orel, which is only 382 kilometres distant from Moscow. In the Ukraine a peasant revolt broke out in the rear of the Red forces. The White counter-revolution derived advantage from the accentuation of the class struggle in the villages, while the peasants rebelled against the compulsory requisitions of their produce.

By the end of April the situation had undergone a radical change to the disadvantage of the Soviet Government. More than five-sixths of Russian territory were in the hands of the Whites, whose forces moved onward from east and south towards Moscow like an irresistible steam-roller. (See Map 1.)

In March 1919, Frunse became Commander-in-Chief of the troops opposing Kolchak on the eastern front; in the middle of April the 5th Red Army, commanded by Tuchachevsky, was added to his forces. Tuchachevsky was in charge of the counterstroke, and he concentrated 36,000 of the 60,000 men comprising the eastern army in Busulug, a small town in the central Volga area, not far from Samara, leaving the 700-kilometre stretch of front held only by a weak line.

He thus gained a decisive tactical superiority at the centre of gravity he had chosen. He broke through the White front and rolled it up. After the battle of Busulug he initiated an advance that is almost unparalleled in military history, for it started from the Volga area, crossed the Urals, and then continued right through Asiatic Russia until it reached Vladivostok. His forces covered a distance of over 8,000 kilometres under conditions of practically continuous action.

On August 13, 1919, Frunse diverged into Turkestan
with a portion of the Eastern Red Army, while Tuchachevsky continued the pursuit of Kolchak with the
2nd and 5th Armies. He took Omsk on November
14; Tomsk fell to him on December 22, and Krasnoyarsk (3,217 kilometres by rail from Samara) on
January 6, 1920. For 247 days the Red forces thus
covered an average of 13 kilometres a day, during
which time they were not merely engaged in continuous
fighting, but had also to scale the steep slopes of the
Ural range and face the icy cold of a Siberian winter.

In January 1920, Kolchak was cut off from the Pacific
coast by a rebellion that broke out in his rear at Irkutsk.
The Czechoslovak Legion concluded an armistice with
the Reds and handed over the gold of the Russian
treasury, which they had captured in Kazan, in return
for a free passage. Kolchak shot himself before the
Soviet troops marched into Irkutsk.

In January Tuchachevsky was recalled from the
eastern front to central Russia, where he was given
charge of the operations against Denikin, who had
occupied Kiev in the summer of the previous year while
the Red forces were chasing Kolchak's men across the
Urals. Denikin's cavalry, led by General Mammontov,
had broken through the Red lines and reached Tambov,
471 kilometres south of Moscow. They laid waste all
the country through which the Soviet troops would have
to march.

The Soviet Government proceeded to create its own

powerful cavalry forces. The first mounted troops had
been raised as far back as the summer and autumn of
1918 by the Revolutionary Council of the southern
army (Stalin, Yegorov and Voroshilov) from Budyonny's guerilla troops, but Trotsky had always so far
opposed the employment of cavalry in the Civil War,
because it had to be recruited mainly from Cossacks,
whose former privileged position made them unreli-
able.

But now Trotsky hurled his slogan at the masses:
"Proletarians, to horse!" Voroshilov was attached as
commissar to Budyonny, the commander of the first
cavalry forces. Therewith he was deprived of his
independent command, and the Revolutionary Council
of War thought they had found occupation for his
individualistic guerilla tendencies which would keep
him out of mischief.

October 9, 1919, was the date of the Red counter-
offensive against Orel, which was captured by Uborevitch. The very first engagements proved Budyonny's
horsemen to be the superiors of the White cavalry, while
the Ukrainian peasantry went over to the Soviet side
once more, since they realized that a Denikin victory
would mean the return of the former landed proprietors.
Makhno's guerilla forces effected a junction with the
Red Army and advanced against Taganrog, on the Sea
of Azov, where Denikin had his headquarters.

The seeds of decay were sown in Denikin's army
when he resorted to conscription in the summer of 1919.

Lenin foresaw the consequences of this step when he
stated on July 4, 1919:

"A general mobilization will finish Denikin off, just
as it finished off Kolchak. So long as his army was a
class one, consisting only of volunteers of an anti-
socialist character, it was strong and reliable. He was
certainly in a position to raise forces more quickly when
he instituted compulsory military levies, but the greater
the size of his army, the less class-conscious it was, and
the weaker it became. The peasants conscripted into
Denikin's forces will serve him in the same way as the
Siberian peasants served Kolchak, that is to say, they
will disorganize his army completely."

Denikin had just started a counter-offensive from the
lower Don area when Tuchachevsky took over the
supreme command of the southern army. The Whites
were able to book some initial successes; then Tuchachevsky executed a deep turning movement which put
him in a position to attack Denikin's right flank at
Tikhoryetsk. Denikin was forced to a disorderly
retreat, and could only manage to put some remnants of
his army on board ship at Novorossiisk, where they
were despatched to join Wrangel in the Crimea. Thus
the Red forces led by Tuchachevsky liquidated Soviet
Russia's two most dangerous opponents, Kolchak and
Denikin.

In October 1919, Trotsky commanded the forces
which beat off General Yudenich's attack on Petrograd.
A 'Government of the North-West' had been formed

in the country to the north-west of the town under the
protectorate of the British General March; this body
had concluded an agreement with Estonia, whose
independence it recognized. General Yudenich, who
commanded the armies of the 'Government of the
North-West,' had troops under his control which
included 70,000 'eaters,' but only 20,000 fighters. He
was accompanied by no fewer than fifty-three former
Tsarist generals, all of whom aspired to posts and
received occupation commensurate with their rank.
But when Yudenich's army was defeated in October
1919, the 'Government of the North-West' ceased to
exist, while the British Fleet, on which he relied for
support, left him in the lurch, and the Estonians did
the same. The remnants of the White forces fled into
Estonia, where they were interned.

In February and March 1920, the forces of the Red
Army suppressed the 'Government of the North'
established in Archangelsk and Murmansk under the
protection of English and American forces commanded
by General Miller. Consequently the spring of 1920
saw the liberation of Soviet Russia from the encircling
ring of hostile armies, the only foes remaining to be
dealt with being the forces of General Wrangel, which
held out in the Crimea. This area was not reconquered
until after the termination of the Polish campaign, when
Frunse accomplished the task.

The year 1920 was taken up by the Polish campaign,
which is the subject of another chapter. Red forces

occupied Georgia in February 1921, and the Kronstadt revolt broke out in the following March. The forces of Baron Ungern Sternberg in the Far East were annihilated in the autumn of 1921, while in October of the same year the pressure exercised by the Red Armies under Uborevitch compelled the Japanese and Americans composing the remaining Entente forces, to evacuate Vladivostok. Therewith the four years of Civil War came to an end.

The Intervention Fiasco.

'Fourteen States' sent forces to Russia to suppress the Socialist Revolution. They included the world's principal Great Powers—Britain, France, America and Japan—which had just succeeded in defeating German imperialism. With them were associated Czechoslovakia, Greece, Poland, Latvia, Finland, Estonia, Yugoslavia, Rumania, Lithuania and Turkey, while we must also include the Germans, who were active in the Ukraine in 1918 and in the Baltic States in 1919. Yet the Bolshevists triumphed over all this array of forces.

The interventionist Powers were divided among themselves by a clash of interests, and could therefore form no homogeneous plan for the conquest of Russia. If Poland had thought fit to attack at the time when Denikin controlled southern Russia and was on the march to Moscow, the Soviets would have been finished, but the reactionary Poles were not interested

in southern Russia. Denikin's forces had to be defeated
before Poland chose to attack Soviet Russia in support
of her Ukrainian vassal, Petliura.

The lack of unity in the camp of the interventionist
Powers was one cause of the non-success of their
intervention. The other cause may be found in the ugly
mood prevailing among the peoples of those lands.

Clemenceau desired to suppress the Soviets by
force of arms, but his own sailors, led by Marty, struck
his weapons out of his hands. Curzon and Churchill
launched an appeal for a crusade against Bolshevism,
but the British workers opposed it, and Lloyd George
adopted a vacillating attitude. Although the interventionist Powers invaded Russian soil with their White
forces, the Soviets had allies of their own in the enemy's
countries. We need only cite the eloquent complaints
which Churchill—then British Minister for War—made
in his speech at the banquet of the Anglo–Russian Club
on July 17, 1919:

"The great success achieved by our assistance shows
that we could have effected a complete restoration in
Russia by now, if the five victorious Great Powers had
given strong and disinterested support from the very
beginning. But there are among us a considerable
number of people who would be unfeignedly glad to see
Kolchak and Denikin, their forces, and all who espouse
their cause, beaten and subjected to the Bolshevist
Government. They would rejoice to see Lenin, Trotsky
and their strange obscure band of Jewish anarchists and

adventurers occupy the mighty throne of the Tsars without resistance or rivals, and add the new tyranny of their
subversive ideas to the despotic methods of the old
régime."

Denikin was the last card on which the Allies staked
their hopes. In the middle of April 1919, they were
giving support to Kolchak, but his defeat 'disappointed'
them. On April 24 Clemenceau sent Kolchak a telegram, in which he assured him that Denikin would be
able to hold his ground as soon as he received help from
the Entente, while the British, French and Rumanian
forces would occupy southern Russia and the Poles
would threaten sufficiently serious danger to the Bolshevists from the west. The French statesman therefore
advised Kolchak to continue his offensive against
Moscow and try to make contact with Denikin on his
left wing.

This telegram must have been but a poor consolation
to Kolchak, whose forced marches at that time were
not directed towards Moscow, but rather towards the
Urals. The last official British assistance received by the
Whites was a sum of £14,500,000 given to Denikin.
Churchill sent the following telegram to Kolchak about
this sum:

"Some time ago the British Government decided to
concentrate their assistance on General Denikin's front.
I am happy to inform you that the Cabinet has agreed
on my recommendation to send General Denikin the
sum of fourteen and a half million pounds for arms

and equipment. The Cabinet is also of my opinion that it would be the most sensible plan to support General Denikin because he is close to Moscow and has occupied the corn and coal-mining centres."

Lloyd George vacillated, but did not become definitely anti-interventionist until the fiasco of intervention was manifest. From the memorandum which he sent to the Versailles Council of Four on March 25, 1919, we may cite the following resounding trumpet-blast:

"The greatest danger I perceive in the present situation is the possibility of Germany uniting her destiny with that of the Bolshevists and placing her wealth, intellect and great organizing capacity at the disposal of the men who dream of conquering the world for Bolshevism by force of arms. This danger is no idle fancy. If Germany goes over to Spartacism, she will inevitably link her fate with that of the Bolshevists. If that takes place, all eastern Europe will be drawn into the maelstrom of the Bolshevist Revolution, and a year hence we shall find ourselves opposed by nearly 3,000,000 men who will be welded by German generals and German instructors into a gigantic army equipped with German machine-guns and ready to undertake an offensive against western Europe."

But the same trumpet sounded a retreat on November 17, 1919, after the heavy defeats inflicted on Denikin and Wrangel. When discussing the Russian question in the House of Commons on that day, Lloyd George said:

"Whenever the armies have marched beyond a certain point in their attacks on Bolshevism, they have failed. It is perfectly obvious that this country, with the enormous burdens cast upon it by the War, cannot undertake the responsibility of financing civil war in Russia indefinitely. Our first concern must be for our own people."

The "concern for our own people" was due to the opposition manifested by British workers and soldiers to the anti-socialist intervention. This opposition, in fact, was the decisive reason for its complete failure. On December 6, 1919, three weeks after Lloyd George's speech in the House of Commons, Lenin said to the 7th Soviet Congress:

"What is the miracle which enabled the Soviets to carry on two years of obstinate warfare, first against the German imperialism then deemed omnipotent, and later against Entente imperialism, and this despite our backwardness, poverty and war-weariness? We deprived the Entente of its soldiers. The victory we won when we forced the withdrawal of English and French troops was the most decisive success we have ever achieved against the Entente. We vanquished their numerical and technical superiority by virtue of the solidarity shown by the workers against imperialist governments."

The intervention was a fiasco because its attempt to incite the internal forces of counter-revolution was carried out with insufficient means. When, therefore, the internal counter-revolution 'failed' and the Allies were 'disappointed,' they were forced to disappoint their White Russian confederates, and so the intervention broke down.

Some Military-Political Problems.

When appraising the military value of the operations in the Civil War, we must beware of mechanical comparison with the standards set by the World War or application of the experiences of the Russian Civil War to future wars fought out between modern mechanized armies.

The number of actual combatants in the Civil War was relatively small in comparison with those who took part in the World War. 'Mass armies' of 100, to 150,000 men were the largest forces which fought on either side in the Civil War. The statistics of the Red Army's General Staff show that the White Guard forces fighting on Russian soil in the summer of 1919, i.e. at the time when they made their greatest efforts, did not number more than 500,000 infantry, 100,000 cavalry, 2,800 machine-guns and 700 cannon. This total of 600,000 men was distributed over three or four theatres of war completely separated from one another.

In view of the better military training and leadership of the Whites, and, moreover, of the higher percentage of experienced officers and N.C.O.s in their ranks provided by a corps of trained men, it was obvious that

the Reds could only win if they had the 'bigger battalions' on their side. The Red Higher Command realized
the possibility of exploiting the advantage of fighting
on inner lines and bringing a numerical superiority to
bear on the enemy at the crucial point, as we may see
from the example afforded by operations in the summer
of 1919, when 172,000 men were concentrated on the
southern front against Denikin's 152,000. The Red
numerical superiority was even more pronounced in the
final operations against Wrangel in the Crimea, when
Frunse's troops were reinforced by formations brought
from the Polish front, so that he was able to take the
field with 143,000 men and 500 guns against Wrangel's
37,220 men and 213 guns. In March 1919, when the
forces opposing each other at Samara, on the eastern
front, were more or less equal in numbers (111,000 Reds
with 379 guns against 113,000 Whites with 200 guns), the
Reds were forced to retreat until the arrival of Tuchachevsky's 5th Army gave them the numerical superiority
needed for victory.

This fact does nothing to detract from the extraordinary heroism shown by the Red forces. An army
welded together in the fire of war and civil war could
be victorious in battle against well-knit formations
composed of officers, non-commissioned officers and
men of the old regular Tsarist army only if its leaders
contrived to exploit the heroism of revolutionary
warriors in combination with tactical superiority at the
decisive strategic centres of gravity.

No retrospective conclusions with regard to the employment of modern mass armies can be drawn from the engagements of the Russian Civil War. This may easily be seen from a comparison of the armies of 150,000 men and their inferior technical equipment with the man-power, running into millions, that provided the armies of the World War. In January 1918, for example, the Entente had 1,480,000 infantry, 74,000 cavalry, 8,900 light guns and 6,800 heavy guns on the western front against the 1,232,000 infantry, 24,000 cavalry, 8,800 field-guns and 5,500 heavy guns of the Germans.

The immense distances covered by the Whites were a special feature of the Russian Civil War. All the largest formations of White Guards were raised on the extreme edges of Russia, where Krasnov, Kolchak and Denikin began their attempted advances on Moscow. The length of their routes of march in the eastern and south-eastern theatres of war varied between 960 kilometres (Taganrog–Moscow) and 2,680 kilometres (Omsk–Moscow). On the European parts of the eastern and south-eastern theatres of war every stretch of railway had to serve 150–250 kilometres of the strategical front. The fronts were therefore excessively long, but in reality practically all operations were concentrated on points of strategic importance and more especially on railway-lines. Consequently advances and retreats of several hundred kilometres in length were not abnormal.

This concentration of operations on the railway-lines bestowed overwhelming importance on the armoured trains. A successful raid by one of these trains might result in the conquest of entire districts. Therein also lies the explanation of the ominous effect that the rebellion of the Czechoslovak Legion exercised on the whole development of the Civil War. But in the course of the years the importance of the railways was offset to some extent by the increased organizational capacity of both sides, whereupon the fronts assumed a more general nature.

Much of the hardest fighting took place in the Volga area, the possession of which was so strenuously contested by both sides. This is easily comprehensible in view of the fact that fifteen railway-lines approach the stream from the west, so that an enemy advancing from the east was able to make use of them as soon as he gained control of the river.

In a civil war the front is everywhere. The man-power reserves of both sides are distributed over the whole country. It must therefore be the endeavour of both belligerents to make active use of the reserves immediately behind the enemy's front line and in the centres of government.

The part of these reserves which includes the lower middle classes of the towns and the peasants is bound to vacillate and develop its own activities in accordance with transient feelings; this is the soil on which guerilla warfare thrives. But other sections of the population immediately behind the front and along the lines of communication will comprise the enemy's loyalest and most resolute adherents, for which reason espionage and counter-espionage assumed extraordinarily large dimensions in the Russian Civil War.

The activities of the White agents were mainly confined to military espionage in the narrow sense of the word and to acts of sabotage; only in exceptional cases did they undertake the organization of counter-revolutionary revolts. The latter type of work was, however, one of the most important tasks of the Red agents, who endeavoured to crown and complete the attacks of the regular Red forces by revolts of workers and peasants in the rear of the Whites.

The direction of Red espionage and counter-espionage rested entirely in the hands of the Cheka or 'Extraordinary Commission for the Suppression of Counter-Revolution.' This body, which was the forerunner of the G.P.U., proved to be the all-seeing eye of the dictatorship of the proletariat during the years of the Civil War.

The Kronstadt Mutiny.

Military intervention was not the hardest blow which the capitalist Powers dealt to the Socialist Revolution. The latter was hit far more severely by the blockade, which was complete enough to stifle all foreign trade, as may be seen by the following figures of imports and exports in millions of pouds:[1]

	1913	1917	1918	1919	1920
Imports	936.6	178.0	11.5	0.5	5.2
Exports	1472.1	56.6	1.8	0.0001	0.7

In this connexion we must note that Tsarist Russia imported from abroad 58 per cent of its industrial machinery and plant and 45 per cent of its agricultural machinery.

3,762 railway bridges, 3,597 road bridges, more than 1,700 kilometres of railway-line, and over 90,000 kilometres of telegraph wires were destroyed in the course of the Civil War. Moreover, the territory in possession of the Soviets was cut off for several years from the Caucasus oil deposits as well as from the most important industrial and agricultural centres for long periods. The consequences of this wholesale destruction hit the Red Army and the Soviet Republic in two directions—on its technical-economic side and on its social-political side.

As Trotsky most aptly remarked, the Bolshevists were compelled to "plunder all Russia" in order to satisfy the army's most elementary needs. Trotsky certainly did not exaggerate, for in 1920 the army consumed 25 per cent of the entire wheat production, 50 per cent of the other grain products, 60 per cent of the fish and meat supplies, and 90 per cent of all the men's boot and shoe wares. Moreover, the clothing supplied to the army was the barest minimum, while the deficiency in

[1] The *poud* is a Russian measure.

equipment was even greater. The combined effects of the blockade and of the separation of the Soviets from the important centres of production were seen in the fact that the war commissariat was unable to provide arms for more than 10 per cent of the men mobilized.

The Bolshevists were forced to commandeer all the peasants' surplus grain in order to ensure the supplies needed to feed the army and the industrial proletariat. The so-called 'requisition squads' and the system of forced quotas which extracted the peasants' last grain stores from their hiding-places and throttled all petty commerce were frequent causes of the peasantry's vacillation to the side of the Whites.

But during the Civil War the peasants' only choice lay between the communist requisition squads and the old landed proprietors, who wanted to deprive them of their land as well as their surplus stores. It was a hard choice, but in the end they decided that the communists were the lesser evil.

After the defeat of the Whites the peasants found themselves faced with another pair of alternatives. They could choose between the communist requisition squads and their own 'independent economic system.' In this case the choice was easy, and their opposition to the communists began to stiffen.

The policy of compulsory requisitioning of all peasants' surplus products by agents of the dictatorship of the proletariat was a war measure which conflicted with all the theoretical conceptions held by the greatest of socialists. "War and destruction forced 'war communism' upon us," wrote Lenin in his pamphlet on the natural produce tax in 1921. "This policy was not and never could be in accordance with the economic mission of the proletariat. It was merely a provisional measure. The correct policy of a proletariat which has achieved a dictatorship in a land of small middle classes is one that induces the peasant to exchange his produce for the products of industry which he needs. This is the food policy which harmonizes with the mission of the proletariat, and the only one capable of consolidating the basis of socialism and securing a complete socialist victory."

When the Civil War came to an end in the autumn of 1920, the Bolshevists failed to realize the right way to effect a speedy abolition of the methods of 'war communism,' investigate their relations with the peasantry, and remould them on socialistic principles. Moreover, a consequence of the Civil War and of the absolute power placed in the hands of the communists by the necessities of warfare was manifested in the bureaucratic excrescences that flaunted themselves in all spheres of society—in the Soviets, trade unions, economic administration and throughout the machinery of government.

This bureaucratism found an extraordinarily fruitful soil in the backward state of the Russian people. Bureaucracy, as Lenin ascertained, developed particularly luxurious growths by reason of the methods used by 'war communism.'

"We could not reorganize our industries when we were blockaded and besieged on all sides," he wrote. "We dared not call a halt to 'war communism'; in our despair we dared not shrink from extreme measures. But the measures which are an essential condition of victory in a blockaded land and a besieged fortress revealed their negative side in the spring of 1921, when the last White Guard forces had been driven off the soil of the Union of Socialist Soviet Republics. In a besieged fortress any and every exchange of goods must be stopped. Such a state of affairs may be endured for three years if the masses are particularly heroic, but meanwhile the impoverishment of the petty producers will increase. Bureaucratism has now revealed itself as a legacy of the state of siege and a superstructure built on the bodies of the broken, crushed petty producers."

In these words Lenin defined the facts of the retention of the policy of 'war communism,' which caused the Kronstadt Mutiny in March 1921.

The social-political essence of the four years' Civil War shaped it as a struggle between the working class and the bourgeoisie for power over the masses of lower middle class individuals and, above all, over the peasantry. The fact that the bourgeoisie relied on the assistance of military formations sent by foreign imperialist powers gave this class war the characteristics of a national war of independence. The entire mass of the industrial proletariat was actively on the side of the Bolshevists during this civil war, while the rest of the proletarian and semi-proletarian classes gave some measure of support to the dictatorship of the proletariat, although with considerable vacillations.

The industrial proletariat also vacillated during the Kronstadt Mutiny. Its sympathies inclined to the cause of the men of Kronstadt, whom it supported openly by means of mass strikes in Petrograd and other large towns. As the bonds between the dictatorship of the proletariat and the peasantry had been severed, the Bolshevists now found themselves isolated for the first time since their victory in October 1917. But the machinery of state was shown to be firmly in their hands, while the ties between the peasant army and the village populations were loosened by years of civil war and the continual transference of the Red forces from one theatre of war to another. The army proved itself a reliable instrument in the hands of the Bolshevist leaders when they were forced to quell the Kronstadt Mutiny.

The note of this mutiny was sounded by mass strikes of the Petrograd workers. The Russian industrial workers had never quite lost their contact with the villages; when the pick of these workers were fighting on all fronts during the Civil War, their places in the factories were taken by a continual stream of labour pouring in from the villages; consequently the demands of the striking workmen brought a number of peasant problems into the foreground with them. On February 27, 1921, the Petrograd Strike Committee issued the following proclamation :

"The whole policy of the government must undergo a thorough change, and first and foremost the workers and peasants must have their freedom. They do not want to follow Bolshevist leaders; they want to decide their own lot for themselves. You must therefore put forward the following demands urgently and in an organized way:

"The release of all socialist and non-party workers who have been arrested.

"The abolition of the state of siege.

"Freedom of speech, the press, and meeting for all working classes.

"Free voting in new elections for the factory committees, trade unions and Soviets."

The wage problem was as acute a question as the ugly mood of the workers. The average workman's real wage was barely a third of his pre-War wage. In 1913 a factory worker generally earned something like 22 gold roubles a month, but his total monthly income in 1918 (wages plus food ration) had only the purchasing value of 8.99 pre-War roubles. In 1920 this purchasing value had sunk to 7.12 roubles, and in the spring of 1921 it was only 6.95 roubles, i.e. only 31.6 per cent of the pre-War wage.

The mutiny at Kronstadt broke out on March 3, 1921, at the time when a wave of strikes spread from Petrograd over the whole of Russia.

The sailors manning the fleet at Kronstadt were mainly recruited from lads of the Ukrainian peasantry.

In its social-political aspect the Kronstadt Mutiny was therefore a peasant revolt, supported by part of the urban proletariat. In the course of the disturbances the peasants ejected the Bolshevist Soviets whenever they could institute mass action, organize military formations and obtain possession of arms.

The proclamations issued by the Kronstadt sailors contained many political and economic demands which were brought forward on behalf of the industrial pro-letariat in precisely the same way that the demands of the peasantry were incorporated in the strike manifestoes of the Petrograd workers. From this we may note that the workers exercised a strong influence on the mutineers. A large number of Kronstadt communists and practically the entire population of the island—composed mainly of fishermen and metal workers—took part in the rising. From a resolution passed by the 1st and 2nd brigades of battleship crews we may note the following sections:

(8) Abolition of the requisition squads.

(9) Equal rations for all workers except those engaged in unhealthy occupations.

(11) Liberty for the peasants to cultivate all the land in their own fashion; permission to own privately all the live stock they can keep without the employment of hired labour.

(15) Permission to carry on home industries not involving employment of hired labour.

The 13th issue of the *News Bulletin of the Provisional Revolutionary Committee of Sailors, Red Army Men and Workers of the Town of Kronstadt*, published on March 15, 1921, also states:

"All the peasant workers have been declared exploiters and enemies of the people. The enterprising Communists have taken the work of destruction in hand and are beginning to establish Soviet economy in the form of agricultural estates that are to be the property of the State, which is the new landed proprietor. Communist agricultural economy has been introduced everywhere, and the Communists have taken the best land for this purpose and placed a heavier, harder burden on the backs of the poor peasants than the old landed proprietors did in their time."

The same number of this bulletin contains a quotation from a speech made by a peasant at the 8th Congress of Soviets held in December 1920. "All is well, but . . . the land belongs to us, but the bread from it is yours; the rivers belong to us, but the fish to you; the forests belong to us, but the wood from them to you."

The political aims of the Kronstadt Mutiny may be ascertained from a leading article in the fifth issue of the same bulletin, which states:

"Here in Kronstadt was laid the corner-stone of the Third Revolution, which freed the working masses from their last remaining fetters and opened the way to the construction of a socialist state. The present revolution will allow the working masses freely to elect

their own Soviets, which can then do their work without pressure from the Party and transform the bureaucratic trade unions into free organizations that will
unite the workers, peasants and intelligentsia."

The 10th Bolshevist Party Congress was in session at
Moscow when the news of the Kronstadt Mutiny came
through. At first the assembled delegates thought
Kronstadt was going to provide another 'Czechoslovak Insurrection' and a beacon to light another civil
war and provoke further intervention. The spectre of
a new civil war cast its shadow over the whole Soviet
Republic, for the exiled leaders of the Menshevist,
Social Revolutionary, Cadet and Monarchist parties
all sent their good wishes to the Kronstadt mutineers.

An army was despatched to Kronstadt under
Tuchachevsky's command. Several hundred delegates
volunteered for service as officers and commissars in the
contingents that were to liquidate the mutiny. Then,
while the mutineers sent telegram after telegram to
"Lenin, the incorruptible," Tuchachevsky's forces
advanced from Krasnaya Gorka across the treacherous
ice of the Gulf of Finland which the spring gales were
breaking up. On the night of March 16 they overpowered the sleeping Kronstadt, which had deemed any
form of attack from the sea an impossibility. More
executions followed, the rebels were shot as mutineers
and counter-revolutionaries, but the economic points
of their programme were embodied in the resolutions
of the 10th Party Day, which advocated the replacement

of the quota system by a produce tax, and were realized later in the New Economic Policy (Nep). The political demands of the men of Kronstadt (which, despite their vagueness, aimed at the restoration of Soviet democracy) attained, however, only to a partial and incomplete realization. Lenin, indeed, began the struggle against bureaucracy, but owing to his illness and premature death this 'legacy' of Tsarist backwardness and the Civil War spread like a plague.

The swift liquidation of the Kronstadt Mutiny showed the Bolshevist Party wherein the weakness of any mass movement directed against the party in power lay.

The Bolshevist Party had acquired a monopoly of authority; it was the only organized force which represented the Soviet Russian proletariat. That was its strength, but therein also lay the seeds of its decay.

On the occasion of the celebration of his fiftieth birthday on April 23, 1920, Lenin took the opportunity to address a meeting of the active members of the Moscow branch of the Party in the following terms:

"Even to-day our Party might, under certain circumstances, fall into a very dangerous position. It might fall into the position of a man who has grown presumptuous. Everyone knows that the decline and fall of political parties is often preceded by some circumstance which gives these parties the chance to grow presumptuous. Permit me to conclude with the hope that under no circumstances will our party ever become a presumptuous party."

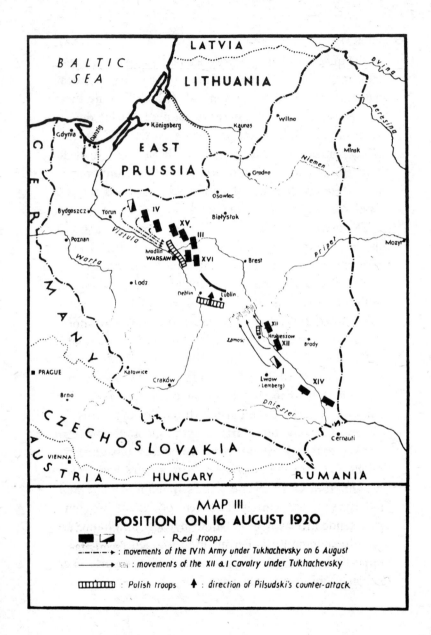

MAP III
POSITION ON 16 AUGUST 1920

■ ◿ ⌒ : Red troops

—·—·—·→ : movements of the IVth Army under Tukhachevsky on 6 August

——→ : movements of the XII & I Cavalry under Tukhachevsky

▯▯▯▯▯▯ : Polish troops ♠ : direction of Pilsudski's counter-attack

Map labels: BALTIC SEA, LATVIA, LITHUANIA, Gdynia, Danzig, Königsberg, Kaunas, Wilno, Dvina, Beresina, EAST PRUSSIA, Grodno, Niemen, Minsk, Osowiec, Białystok, Mozyr, Bydgoszcz, Torun, IV, XV, III, Pripet, Poznan, Warta, Vistula, Modlin, WARSAW, XVI, Brest, Łodz, Deblin, Lublin, XII, Hrubieszow, XII, Brody, Zamosc, PRAGUE, Katowice, Kraków, Lwow (Lemberg), I, XIV, Brno, Dniester, CZECHOSLOVAKIA, VIENNA, AUSTRIA, HUNGARY, RUMANIA, Cernauti, GERMANY

Chapter Four

Military Operations.

Frederick the Great once clothed his foreign policy in a garb of bad Latin. *Prevenire, non preveniri,* he said, meaning to imply thereby that it is better to spring a surprise attack on the enemy than to let him get his blow in first.

Pilsudski acted on this maxim in the spring of 1920. Dr. Vaclav Lipinski, for many years Polish ambassador in Berlin, avows this more or less unashamedly in an article entitled "The Great Marshal," which appeared as a preface to the German translation of Pilsudski's *Memoirs.* In this he wrote:

"The new year of 1920 was to bring about a radical change in the existing war situation. The Bolshevists made strenuous preparations for a surprise attack on Poland after they had defeated the armies of Kolchak, Denikin and Yudenich that opposed the Revolution. The essential objective of this surprise attack was evident; they intended to destroy Poland in order to join hands with Germany, still shaken by revolutionary fermentation, and thus light the fire of communist revolution throughout Europe. Joseph Pilsudski, who was in

supreme command of the Polish forces, decided to
anticipate the enemy's onslaught by an offensive of his
own, since attack is the most effective form of defence.

"Since the first information he received reported a
concentration of Russian forces in the Ukraine, he
resolved to deal his blow in the same direction and
combine this plan with political operations far-reaching
in their purpose. In order to weaken Russia and
strengthen the forces of her foes, Pilsudski therefore
signed on April 22, 1920, a military agreement with
Petliura, the military and political leader of the
Ukrainian independence movement; four days later he
launched severe attacks which enabled him to destroy
two Russian armies and enter Kiev on May 7."

Lipinski's assertion that Soviet Russia was making
'strenuous preparations' for war against Poland in the
spring of 1920 is refuted by the fact that only very weak
Russian forces were stationed on the line of her Polish
frontier. On April 25, 40,000 men (Polish regulars and
Petliura's formations) advanced into the Ukraine, but
the Poles had already occupied the two frontier towns
of Mosyr and Rechnize on March 6.

After their occupation the Revolutionary Council of
War of the Soviet Republic ordered Budyonny's cavalry
army, then in the Caucasus, to proceed to the Ukraine.
But these forces were still on the march when Pilsudski
launched his great offensive.

Only the scanty troops of the 12th Red Army,
amounting in all to 12,000 men, were then in the

Ukraine. Further southward, in the vicinity of the Bessarabian frontier, the 14th Red Army was already involved in a series of engagements with Petliura's troops and 'wild' Rumanian formations. The 12th Army was thrown back across the Dnieper, and the Poles took Kiev, which then changed its form of government for the fifteenth time since the Revolution.

The Soviet authorities did not despatch any large forces to the Polish frontier until Pilsudski opened hostilities. At the beginning of 1920 they had even offered the Poles peace terms far more favourable than those envisaged by the Entente. But Pilsudski dreamed of the 'pre-1722' frontiers (i.e. those obtaining before the First Partition of Poland), which would have given him a part of the Ukraine, all East Prussia, Lithuania, and White Russia, and half of Latvia for the Greater Poland on which his aspirations were bent.

As Trotsky has made clear in his work *On Military Doctrine*, the fact that Soviet Russia was obviously on the defensive "contributed in very large measure to the work of rallying to our side the public opinion of numerous bourgeois intellectuals as well as that of the workers and peasants."

The Revolutionary Council of War decided to form two army groups for the offensive planned for the Polish campaign. One was to be employed on the 'western front' and to advance on Warsaw from White Russia along a route enabling it to cover its flank by the Lithuanian and East Prussian frontiers, while the other

was to form the 'south-western front,' and march on
Lublin after recapturing Kiev. The operations on this
south-western front were to be co-ordinated with those
on the western front.

Tuchachevsky was appointed Commander-in-Chief
of the western front; Smilga accompanied him as
member of the Revolutionary Council of War, with
Muklevitch as Staff Commissar. The component forces
of the western front included the 4th Army (commanded
by Sergeyev), the 15th Army (commanded by Kork,
with Lashevitch as member of the Revolutionary
Council of War), the 3rd Army (Yakir) and the 16th
Army (Pyatakov as member of the Revolutionary
Council of War).

The Commander-in-Chief on the south-western front
was Yegorov, who also led the 12th Army. Stalin was
the member of the Revolutionary Council of War on
this front, which included, in addition to the 12th Army,
the 1st Calvary Army (commanded by Budyonny, with
Voroshilov as Commissar) and the 14th Army (Uborevitch), which operated on the Bessarabian frontier.

In order to co-ordinate the military operations of
both army groups, the Revolutionary Council of War
decided that the south-western forces (with the exception of the 14th Army) should be subordinated to the
Commander-in-Chief of the western front as soon as
the latter had advanced as far as the meridian of Brest-
Litovsk. This arrangement was a compromise, for
Tuchachevsky had requested the immediate sub-

ordination of both armies of the south-western front to his command, in order to ensure unity of action. But S. S. Kamenev, who was then the supreme commander of all the armed forces of the Soviet Union, decided upon this temporary solution of the difficulty, because considerable friction had existed between Tuchachevsky and the commanders of the south-western front (Yegorov, Stalin and Voroshilov) ever since the Czechoslovak Insurrection in the summer of 1918.

The Revolutionary Council of War ordered troops from almost all parts of Russia to the Polish front as soon as Pilsudski opened hostilities. Until April 1920 practically no forces had been sent to this area.

From December 1919 to April 1920 the region destined to become the western front was occupied only by three infantry divisions and three brigades; on the south-western front, i.e. in the sector where Pilsudski claimed to have noticed such large concentrations of forces that he deemed his *prevenire* to be an indispensable measure of national defence, there was, in January 1920, only a single infantry division. In subsequent months the following formations were sent to the future Polish theatre of war from the former northern front, the Ural military district, the Tula military circuit, the eastern, Caucasus and southern fronts:

To the western front two infantry divisions and two infantry brigades in April, five infantry divisions and two infantry brigades in May, three infantry divisions and three cavalry brigades in June, making a total of ten infantry divisions, five infantry brigades and three cavalry brigades.

To the south-western front five cavalry divisions in April (Budyonny), and three infantry divisions in May and June.

These figures are the best refutation of any assertion that the Soviet Republic cherished offensive intentions against Poland before Pilsudski began hostilities.

Tuchachevsky has given us the following sketch of Soviet Russia's situation at this time in his work *The Advance beyond the Vistula*, which is an abbreviated version of the series of lectures he delivered at the War Academy from February 7–10 :

"Kolchak had been finished off in the east and Denikin in the Caucasus. Wrangel's base 'of operations in the Crimea was the only territory still occupied by the Whites. All operations in the north and west were terminated, with the exception of those on the Polish front. A peace treaty had already been concluded with Latvia. Poland's action therefore came at a time that was comparatively favourable to us."

Although the greater number of Tuchachevsky's forces were still on the way to him on May 20, he launched an attack on Smolensk on that day. Pilsudski maintains in his book *The Year 1920*, written as a reply to Tuchachevsky's work above-mentioned, that in this May offensive "Tuchachevsky's principal mistake (which doomed his great plans to failure in advance), was based on his erroneous estimate of his own and his opponent's forces, which he made without taking any account of his opposite number who commanded the troops on the other side."

This criticism shows that Pilsudski mistook the objectives Tuchachevsky set before him when he made his advance in the Smolensk area. He did not desire to force a decision there, and indeed could not have done so, since he had only received half the troops assigned to his command. His real aim was to relieve the pressure on the south-western front in order to permit the recapture of Kiev and the advance of the 12th and Budyonny's armies on Lublin, so that the forces of the south-west would not be too far from his left flank when he began his impending western front offensive.

Tuchachevsky achieved this minor result with his May offensive, for while he was fighting heavy rear-guard actions in the north, Yegorov counter-attacked on June 5. Budyonny's cavalry broke through the enemy's lines, and the 12th and 14th Armies followed in his wake. The Polish forces beat a precipitate retreat; on June 8 Budyonny took Zhitomir. Kiev was recaptured on June 12; on June 25 Brody was occupied. But meanwhile the situation on the south-western front had grown somewhat critical, for Wrangel had started a victorious northward advance from the Crimea on June 6 and was thus diverting reinforcements from the south-western front since they had to be sent to deal with him.

By the beginning of July Tuchachevsky had concentrated sufficient forces to take the offensive. The 48,837 infantry and 3,456 cavalry at his disposal when he made his first advance in May, had now reached totals of 80,942 and 10,521 respectively, distributed as follows:

The 4th Army comprised about 14,000 infantry and cavalry, the 15th about 26,000, the 3rd about 20,000, and the 16th about 25,000. There was also the 57th infantry division, composed of some 6,000 infantry and cavalry, which was a 'special division' operating independently on the left flank of the south-western front. This was afterwards known as the Mosyrz Group, because of its advance in the direction of Mosyrz.

The total artillery armament of the south-western front consisted of 395 guns.

Tuchachevsky stated that his forces also included 68,725 men for whom no arms were available, so that he could employ them only as replacements for front wastage.

Pilsudski estimated the enemy forces opposing him in White Russia at the higher figure of about 200,000 men. The statistics of the equipment and commissariat departments of the General Staff of the Soviet Union give a total of 795,645 men and 150,572 horses employed on the western front during the Polish campaign, and Pilsudski assumes that the Red Higher Command were able to send rather more than 25 per cent of the total man-power of this front into action. It must be noted, however, that he reckoned the percentage of men in the Polish Army that could go into action as only from 12 to 15, "on account of their inferior discipline and Polish weakness and cowardice."

Pilsudski estimates the forces commanded by General Szepycky on the same sector as Tuchachevsky at not more than 100,000 to 120,000 men. He also believes that he had between 120,000 and 180,000 under his own command when he started his counter-offensive in August, this great latitude in his estimate being explicable, as he complainingly asserts, "by the great confusion prevailing at the time." But undoubtedly it would be wise to treat all the statistics of both belligerents with the greatest reserve.

In June Pilsudski wanted to "liquidate Budyonny quickly," because Tuchachevsky's reverse in May led him to believe that he need not anticipate an immediate Russian offensive in the north. He therefore transferred considerable forces to the south.

"I did not attach any great importance to Budyonny's cavalry," he wrote, "and thought their victories in previous Soviet theatres of war were due rather to internal disintegration of their opponents' forces than to any real value in their fighting methods." Consequently Pilsudski did not devote his attention to his northern front again until after all his efforts to defeat Budyonny had failed, i.e., shortly before the opening of Tuchachevsky's offensive. He then left the operations against Budyonny in charge of Rydz-Smigly, "who, like almost everyone else at that time, did not take the enemy's cavalry seriously."

On July 4 Tuchachevsky launched an attack in the sector between the Beresina and the northern Dvina. He massed the 4th, 15th and 3rd Armies on his right wing, thus obtaining an enormous numerical superiority at the point he had chosen for the centre of his operations. Attacking 30,000 Poles with 50,000 infantry and 10,000 cavalry (the 2nd Cavalry Army, commanded by Gay), he broke through the Polish front, and the Soviet troops then advanced westwards in the direction of Warsaw.

Vilna was taken on July 14; on the 19th the ancient fortress of Grodno fell; on the 27th the Russians were in Ossovetz. Pilsudski then thought to deliver a counter-stroke against Tuchachevsky's left flank from the Brest-Litovsk area; on July 30, General Sikorski, who commanded the forces defending the fortress, informed him that he could hold out for ten days. But Brest-Litovsk fell on August 1, two days later, and Bialystok was taken the same day.

Pilsudski has given us the following description of the advance of the Red Armies and the impression they made on the Polish forces and the entire Polish Republic:

"Tuchachevsky's troops advanced continuously as soon as the way was clear for the 4th Army and the cavalry. One day they were only about 20 kilometres away from Warsaw and its environs, i.e., only a normal day's march. This unceasing, wormlike advance of a

huge enemy horde, which went on for weeks, with
spasmodic interruptions here and there, gave us the
impression of something irresistible rolling up like some
terrible thunderclouds that brooked no opposition. The
pressure of this approaching thunderstorm broke the
joints of the machinery of state, weakened all our
characters and took the heart out of our soldiers. By
this march on Warsaw, which originated undoubtedly
in his will and energy, Tuchachevsky gave proof that he
had developed into a general far above the average
commonplace commander."

Pilsudski "then came to a decision contrary to all
logic and the sound principles of warfare." He with-
drew a number of formations from the Polish southern
front, leaving only two-and-a-half infantry divisions to
oppose the 12th Red Army and Budyonny's cavalry.
He planned his counter-offensive on the theoretical
assumption that these Soviet forces did not exist.

In this fashion he concentrated over twenty divisions
against the Russians of the western front, fifteen of
which were destined to play the passive rôle of defenders
of Warsaw. His task was rendered possible and
lightened by the fact that, despite the boycott initiated
by the German workers, considerable artillery material
had reached him from France.

Pilsudski denies to the French any part in his victory
over the Soviet forces, and ascribes all his successes to
the energy and skill displayed by himself and his Polish
co-operators. "It was owing to the extraordinary

energy evinced by General Sosnovski in the Warsaw
area that the artillery came into the picture in a strength
hitherto unknown in our war. It approximated closely
to the ideal evolved by the experiences of the World
War. With this artillery we were able to develop a
proper drum-fire."

When the French artillery served by French officers
under the command of General Sosnovski had
relieved Pilsudski of the greater part of his anxiety for
Warsaw, he concentrated five and a half divisions in
the Deblin-Lublin area, with the intention of despatch-
ing them against Tuchachevksy's unguarded left flank
in the direction of Brest-Litovsk.

Despite their continuous advance, the Russians on
the western front were in a critical position. Both wings
of the main mass were left in the air. The 4th Army,
which operated on the right flank in conjunction with
Gay's strong cavalry forces and on August 5 had received orders to turn off southwards and advance in the
Medlin-Warsaw direction, continued its march in a
north-westerly direction towards the Polish Corridor,
thereby losing touch with the Higher Command. In his
book Pilsudski quotes the witticism of a French officer,
who said that "instead of reaching Warsaw, the 4th
Russian Army fought against the Treaty of Versailles
rather than against Poland."

At dawn on August 16 Pilsudski launched his
counter-offensive from the Deblin–Lublin area. "This
illogical operation which ran counter to all sane

principles of warfare" led to complete success because the forces of the Red south-western armies failed to come into action. Pilsudski found his attacking forces opposed only by a few thousands of men belonging to the 'Mosyrz Group,' which was broken up into very small units forming a broad but very loose cordon against Deblin-Lublin. These retired in disorder when the Polish divisions fell upon them.

Pilsudski's troops met with practically no resistance for the first three days of their offensive. The marshal, who took personal charge of operations, "suspected traps everywhere," "thought he was in some enchanted fairyland" and "saw mysteries and riddles everywhere."

On August 18 Pilsudski was back in Warsaw, where he gave orders for a general advance along the whole line. On the same day Tuchachevsky ordered a general retreat, but "the commander of the 4th Red Army disobeyed orders and began a further advance in the direction of East Prussia." The remaining Red Army formations streamed back in disorder to their original positions between the Beresina and the northern Dvina, while the 2nd Cavalry Army and parts of the 4th Army that had advanced too far westwards were forced on to East Prussian soil and interned in Germany until the end of hostilities.

An armistice came into force on October 12, when the Soviet forces were in occupation of the line that now forms the frontier between the two countries, and on

March 18, 1921, a peace treaty between Poland and Soviet Russia was signed at Tallinn.

Tuchachevsky's charges against Stalin, Yegorov and Voroshilov.

Tuchachevsky attributes the collapse of the Russian offensive to the fact that the forces of the south-western front in general and the 1st Cavalry Army in particular were induced by Stalin and Voroshilov to disobey the Commander-in-Chief's orders. Instead of acting on his instructions to concentrate in the Samosz-Hrubezov area, in readiness for an advance on Lublin, they continued their march on Lwow. He sums up the situation at the opening of the Polish offensive as follows:

"The Poles effected a daring but sound regrouping of their forces; leaving Galicia to take its chance, they concentrated all their strength for their main attack on the decisive western front. At that critical moment our troops were dispersed and moving in various directions. Our left wing, i.e. the groups composing our south-western front, was a continual source of anxiety to the western front in this respect. Anticipating that the Cavalry Army would be at the disposal of the western front at any moment and that we would be able to effect a junction with it, we planned the formation of a strong group, which was to march on Lublin while we concentrated the main forces of the 12th Army and 1st Cavalry Army there. If this had been done in good

time, our army group there would have threatened
danger to the Poles, in which case they would not have
dared to risk an attack from the Deblin-Lublin area,
because they would then have been in a very critical
position. Even if the advance of the Cavalry Army had
been to some extent delayed, the Polish forces would
still have been exposed to the danger of complete and
inevitable defeat, because our victorious cavalry forces
would have taken them in the rear."

In amplification of Tuchachevsky's statement we
must add that according to Pilsudski there were only
16,000 Polish troops to bar the way of the 35,000 men
composing the 12th Army and the Cavalry Army, if
they had advanced on Lublin. But after the fall of
Brody on June 25 Stalin and Voroshilov gave orders for
the cavalry to turn off in the direction of Lwow.
"Worst of all," observes Tuchachevsky, "our victorious
Cavalry Army became involved in severe fighting at
Lwow in those days, wasting time and frittering away
its strength in engagements with infantry strongly
entrenched in front of the town and supported by cavalry
and strong air squadrons."

Budyonny even continued his senseless attacks on the
Lwow fortifications for five days after the opening of
Pilsudski's offensive. He did not order his weakened
forces to march on Lublin 'until it was too late.'

Pilsudski, who was Tuchachevsky's great opposite
number and conqueror in the Polish theatre of
war, makes the following criticism of his opponent's

strictures on the commanders of the south-western
front:

"If Tuchachevsky counted on co-operation with the
Russian forces in the south, he ought to have awaited
the development of their operations there and supported
them when necessary. But as soon as he made up his
mind to advance to the Vistula without reckoning on
support from the south, he had no right to complain
later on of lack of that same support."

Herein Pilsudski overlooks the fact that Tuchachevsky was not in supreme command of all the Soviet
forces, and was thus unable to direct the movements of
the armies of the south-western front in accordance
with his own desires. By virtue of the agreement
reached between him and S. Kamenev, the forces on the
south-western front were to be subordinated to him
after the capture of Brest-Litovsk; although his troops
took this fortress on August 1, it was not until August
11 that Kamenev instructed their commanders "to
regroup their formations and despatch the Cavalry
Army to Zamosc-Hrubeszov at once." Yegorov's 12th
Army was placed under Tuchachevsky's command on
August 13, but, like the Cavalry Army, it was induced
by Stalin and Voroshilov to disobey these orders.

Apart from the above reservations, Pilsudski is of
opinion that a concentration of the cavalry in the
Zamosc-Hrubeszov area would have brought his whole
plan of operations to naught. "The elimination of the
strong battle force that the enemy possessed in Budy-

onny's cavalry was a basic condition for the successful execution of my plan," he writes. "Our south-western front had to be abandoned to its fate. I did not deem it impossible for the cavalry forces which had done us so much damage to resume their forward movement. Their correct line of march was the one which would have brought them nearer to the Russian main armies commanded by Tuchachevsky, and this would also have threatened the greatest danger to us. Everything seemed black and hopeless to me, the only bright spots on the horizon being the failure of Budyonny's cavalry to attack my rear and the weakness displayed by the 12th Red Army."

Pilsudski began his offensive with only these "bright spots on the horizon." But he admitted in advance that he "realized that the weakened forces of the southern front would not be in a position to hold the enemy opposing them, and therefore instructed the 6th Army to retreat slowly on Lwow in the event of any pressure from the Russians. But in the event of Budyonny turning northward, I ordered our cavalry to co-operate with the best infantry division in those parts in pursuing him and to delay his advance at any cost."

Even Tuchachevsky did not lay such strong emphasis on the decisive importance of an attack by the Russian cavalry on the flank of the Polish shock troops. Pilsudski planned to entice Budyonny still further into the environs of Lwow by the retreat of his own troops, but he also gave them strict orders to delay the

Russian cavalry leader's northward advance at any cost.

Pilsudski goes still further, however. In view of the danger threatening him, he resorts to "an extremely daring action." "By withdrawing the 1st and 3rd Legionary Divisions from the southern front," he writes, "I opened the way for Budyonny's cavalry to attack us."

This was, in fact, the "illogical" element in Pilsudski's plan of attack "which ran counter to all sane principles of warfare." But on August 15 he was able to note with triumph that "Budyonny's Cavalry Army developed activities in the south, and our 6th Army began to fall back on Lwow under the pressure he exercised." These operations guaranteed him more or less against the risk of the Red Cavalry falling upon his flank and rear, so that he was able to begin his offensive on August 16 with an easier conscience.

What are the arguments with which the commanders of the Russian south-western front—Stalin, Voroshilov and Yegorev—defend their action?

At first they made no attempt to defend it. It was not until Stalin was involved in his struggle with Trotsky some years later that he asserted that the whole plan of campaign drawn up by Tuchachevsky and Trotsky was utterly wrong in its conception and that "it was based on a purely military point of view which ignored the political aspect." His complaint was that this plan of campaign, based on an encircling of Warsaw initiated

from the north, involved a march through agricultural
areas, whereas the great industrial districts lay in the
line of an advance through the territory to the south
and south-west of Warsaw.

But Stalin's theory is not exactly strengthened by the
fact that Lwow put up a stiff resistance to the advance
of the Red Armies of the south-west, despite its large
proletarian population. Moreover, any Red Army
advancing on Lodz across territory south of Warsaw
would have been in danger of flank attacks from north
and south, i.e. from strongly fortified Warsaw and from
the fortress of Cracow, which would have gripped it as
if between pincers and crushed it.

Tuchachevsky's plan was based on the idea that the
wide sweep of his right wing would enable it to derive
support from a friendly Lithuania and a Germany
containing a strong working-class movement. But in
any case a subordinate commander cannot permit a
whole plan of campaign to fail merely because he
does not approve of it and prefers to wage a war of his
own.

In reality neither Stalin nor Voroshilov were moti-
vated by their desire to apply "scientific revolutionary
theories" in the year 1920. The real reason for their
actions was the old feud and rivalry between Tuchachevsky and the commanders of the south-western
forces, to which we may add the old guerilla elements in
their blood. Their plan to capture Lwow was not
evolved until after the fall of Brody. "Lwow is so near

—barely a hundred kilometres off our route," they said. "Come on! Let's take it!"

Tuchachevsky, in his book, draws a comparison between the conduct of the chiefs of the south-western front and the behaviour of General Rennenkampff at the battle of Tannenberg in 1914. He amplified this comparison in greater detail in his lectures to the War Academy and accused those leaders of deliberate treachery. At that time, however, Voroshilov was only an insignificant commander of a military district in the Caucasus.

There are, indeed, certain resemblances between General Rennenkampff's behaviour in 1914 and the conduct of the chiefs of the south-western front, who are to-day the heads of the Soviet Government and army. In August 1914 the Russians invaded East Prussia with two armies, with a northern one under Rennenkampff's command, which entered German territory from the east, while Samsonov led the forces attacking from the south. The German Higher Command decided to denude the front opposed to Rennenkampff of practically all its troops, in order to try for a decisive victory over Samsonov in the south. General Max Hoffmann, who played a leading part in the battle, gives the following description of the critical situation of the German forces and Rennenkampff's conduct, which made the German victory possible, in his book: *The War of Neglected Opportunities*:

"No one, however ignorant of the art of war, could

fail to see that it was impossible to transfer two army corps from the northern to the southern front; no one could assume that General Rennenkampff would remain inactive when he received news of the German retreat on the morning of the 21st. Hindenburg's predecessor, Prittwitz, could not have stood the strain on his nerves caused during the next few days by that vital question: 'Will Rennenkampff attack or not?'

"General Samsonov sent Rennenkampff order after order to pursue the Germans, but Rennenkampff's army persisted in its incomprehensible immobility. The German commanders therefore despatched two more army corps to the southern front, in order to use them for the decisive battle against Samsonov.

"The question naturally arises why Rennenkampff refused to attack despite the repeated orders Samsonov sent him by wireless. The slightest advance on his part would have prevented the Tannenberg catastrophe.

"I should therefore like to mention the rumour that Rennenkampff refused his assistance on the grounds of personal enmity for Samsonov. That such a personal enmity did exist between the two men I know for a fact; it dated from the battle of Liao-Yang in the Russo-Japanese War, when Samsonov undertook the defence of the Yentai coal-mines with his Siberian Cossack division, but was compelled to evacuate them because Rennenkampff's detachment on the Russian left wing remained inactive despite repeated orders. Witnesses have told me of the hot words that passed between the two leaders at Mukden railway-station after the battle."

The resemblances between the behaviour of Rennen-kampff, which caused the utter annihilation of a Russian army, and the conduct of the chiefs of the south-western front, which led to the loss of an entire cam-paign are certainly most startling. But the factors which finally made Pilsudski's victory possible may be traced to a source which lies deep below all military con-siderations.

"Revolution from Without."

The plan of the Russian advance on Warsaw was based upon the fundamental idea of revolutionary fraternization with the Polish workers and the excitation of revolutionary conflicts in Germany. Tuchachevsky put the question : "Could Europe back up this socialist movement, which the march on Warsaw con-stituted with a revolution in the west?"

He gave the following answer:

"Events say 'Yes.' The German workers manifested open opposition to the Entente. They sent back the railway-wagons filled with arms and food which France had sent to Poland's aid; they refused to unload the French and British ships sent to Danzig with arms and munitions; they caused accidents on the railways, etc. From East Prussia came hundreds and thousands of volunteers, who formed a German rifle brigade under the banner of the Red Army. In England the working classes were also in the grip of a very active revolutionary movement.

"After a war has been lost it is naturally easy to discover political mistakes and blunders. But a 'revolution from without' was a possibility. Capitalist Europe was profoundly shaken, and perhaps the Polish War might have acted as a connecting link between the October Revolution and a revolution in western Europe, if our strategic blunders and our defeat on the battlefield had not made it impossible.

"Our task was difficult, daring and complicated; but the solution of world problems is never an easy task. There is no doubt that the revolution of the Polish workers would have become a reality if we had succeeded in depriving the Polish bourgeoisie of its bourgeois army. The conflagration caused by such a revolution would not have stopped at the Polish frontiers; it would have spread all over Europe like the waters of a wild mountain torrent.

"The Red Army will never forget this experience of 'revolution from without.' If ever Europe's bourgeoisie challenges us to another war, the Red Army will succeed in destroying it. In such a case the Red Army will support and spread the revolution in Europe."

The error in Tuchachevsky's calculations is to be found in his over-optimistic view of the revolutionary situation in Poland, or, to put it better, his underestimate of the national antagonism between the Polish

race and the Great Russians, who had been their
national oppressors for more than a century. This error
does honour to Tuchachevsky, for it arises from his
revolutionary zeal.

E. N. Sergeyev, who commanded the 4th Red Army,
was definitely sceptical in his judgement of the revolutionary sentiments of the Polish workers. In his book
From Dvina to Vistula he wrote:

"The occupants of political chanceries a long way
from the front were the only people who seriously
believed in the possibility of a Polish Revolution. We
in the army had little faith in it, and obviously our
attempt to form a Polish Red Army in Bialystok is
proof enough of the fact that our sources of information gave us too optimistic a view of the situation in
Poland."

The 'political chanceries' must include Lenin's own
'chancery' and the Comintern, which he and Zinoviev
then directed.

Pilsudski gives detailed attention in his book to the
question of 'Revolution from Without' as expounded
by Tuchachevsky.

"Poland," he writes, "was overwhelmed for a
hundred and twenty years by the blessings of alien rule,
which it hated passionately because it was maintained
by the power of alien bayonets. When Tuchachevsky
stretched out his hand to grasp the centre of our national
life, Warsaw, our capital; when his bayonets had done
their work, the only abiding-place for the Soviet

Revolution was on their points, for within Poland it had no value. Yet all the calculations of Tuchachevsky and his country were based on the idea that the bayonets need only give the word, and then there would be a chance for the Soviet Revolution to develop its power in the land it had invaded."

The truth, in any case, must lie somewhere between the views formed on the one hand by the Bolshevists, including Tuchachevsky, and by Pilsudski on the other. Undoubtedly the majority of the Polish peasants, almost all the urban lower middle classes, and even a part of the working classes of Poland sympathized with the nationalistic ideas of the Polish bourgeoisie. Trotsky, who knew Polish history and the mentality of the Polish proletariat well enough to foresee this outcome, opposed the idea of extending the invasion beyond the ethnographical frontiers of Poland, but he was the only member of the Bolshevist Central Committee to champion this point of view. In his work *On Military Doctrine* he goes into some detail on this problem of 'Revolution from Without,' as exemplified by the Polish campaign:

"We over-estimated the revolutionary character of the Polish internal situation. This over-estimate found expression in the extraordinary aggressiveness—or, more correctly, in the failure of that aggressiveness we might have displayed—of our military operations. We just pushed on all too carelessly, and everyone knows the consequences: we were beaten back. In the great class war now taking place, military intervention from without can play but a concomitant, co-operative, secondary

part. Military intervention may hasten the dénouement
and make the victory easier, but only when both the
political consciousness and the social conditions are ripe
for revolution. Military intervention has the same
effect as a doctor's forceps; if used at the right moment,
it can shorten the pangs of birth, but if employed pre-
maturely, it will merely cause an abortion."[1]

[1] In his *Official History of the Communist Party of the Soviet Union*,
Pepov gives the following exposition of Trotsky's standpoint:
"Trotsky would now have us believe that he opposed the march
on Warsaw because he foresaw its disastrous consequences. He even
presumes to draw a parallel between Brest-Litovsk (the Peace Treaty
of 1918) and Warsaw (1920), alleging that Lenin warned the Party
of the danger in 1918 and he (Trotsky) did the same in 1919. In
reality Trotsky was not opposed to the march on Warsaw on the
ground that he considered our forces inadequate, but because his
social democratic prejudices made him averse to the idea of imposing
'revolution from without' on any country. In July 1920, the Central
Committee rejected Trotsky's anti-Bolshevist, Kautskyist proposals
in the most definite fashion."
But to-day Stalin advocates that very point of view which Pepov
attributes to Trotsky. We may remember his conversation on March
3, 1936, with Howard, the president of the American press syndicate
known as the Scrips-Howard newspapers, from which I quote the
following:
"HOWARD: Are you not of opinion that there may be well-
grounded fears in the capitalist countries that the Soviet Union might
decide upon a forcible conversion of other nations to its political
theories?
"STALIN: There is no reason for such fears. You are greatly mistaken if you think the men of the Soviet would ever want to change
the state of any other country by any means, let alone by force.
"HOWARD: Does this declaration of yours imply that the Soviet
Union has in any way renounced its plans and intentions to bring
about a world revolution?
"STALIN: We never had any such plans or intentions.
"HOWARD: It would seem to me, Mr. Stalin, that quite a different
impression has been current in the world for a long time.
"STALIN: That is the result of a misunderstanding.
"HOWARD: A tragic misunderstanding?
"STALIN: No a comic one. Or perhaps a tragi-comic one. It is
nonsense to try to make revolution an article of export. If a country
wants a revolution, it wants to make it for itself; and if it doesn't
want one, there can be no revolution. To state that we want to
bring about revolution in other countries by meddling in their
manner of life is to assert something which is not true and which
we have never put forward."

The march on Warsaw was unable to bring about a revolution in Central Europe because the fact that centuries of oppression at the hands of the Great Russians had left the Polish proletariat not yet sufficiently mature for revolution, coincided with the military blunders associated with the names of Stalin, Voroshilov and Yegorov.

At the moment when the troops of the Red Army crossed the Vistula, the revolutionary centre of gravity was not on that river, but on the Spree and in the Ruhr; it had leapt from Warsaw to Berlin. The internal hypotheses required for a decisive revolutionary conflict between the proletariat and the bourgeoisie had matured in the Germany of 1920. Field-Marshal von Blomberg reviews the situation then existing in Germany in his preface to the German translation of Pilsudski's *Memoirs*[1] in the following words:

"The Russo-Polish War is not merely a matter of interest to soldiers. Its result has a universal historical significance. Its importance for Germany can hardly be over-estimated, for in this war something more than Polish national liberty and the continued existence of the Polish Republic was at stake. In its final aspect it was a question whether the Bolshevist Revolution should penetrate further into Europe and thus impose its rule on Germany as well as other countries. In the Germany of 1920 many of the preliminary conditions essential for such a revolution existed. Poland after a hard struggle hurled Bolshevism back to the land of its birth and

---

[1] *Memoirs of a Polish Revolutionary and Soldier.*

erected a strong barrier against its further westward advance. Thus Poland saved all Europe, including Germany, from collapse."

Lenin was in favour of the military offensive because the march on Warsaw might have hastened the collapse of capitalist Europe and made easier the victories of the German and other European proletariats. After the defeat of the Soviet forces before Warsaw he gave the following explanation in an address delivered on October 2, 1920, at the celebration of the Trade Union Day of the leather industry workers:

"The Versailles Peace Treaty and the whole international system resulting from the Entente's victory over Germany, would have been convulsed if Poland had become a Soviet State and the Warsaw workers had received from Soviet Russia the help they awaited. That is the reason why the advance of the Red Armies on Warsaw developed into an international crisis. It was only a question of a few more days of victorious advance for us, and then we should not have merely captured Warsaw; we should also have shaken the Versailles Peace Treaty to its foundations. That is the international significance of our war with Poland."

Chapter Five

Official history as written in the Soviet Union to-day refuses to admit the part Trotsky played as organizer of the Red Army's victories, and depicts Stalin as the greatest military leader of the Civil War. In Pepov's historical work we find:

"The high honour of having organized the victories of the Red Army falls first and foremost to the Party and to its leader, Lenin. Lenin's best and most loyal helper in the military sphere was Comrade Stalin. It was Comrade Stalin who in the autumn of 1918, played a leading part in the brilliant defence of Tsaritsyn against General Krasnov, who was then the Soviet Government's most serious opponent. In those days Tsaritsyn served as a wedge between the two main groups of White Guard forces in the south and east.

"In the first months of 1919 it was the forceful work of Comrade Stalin which brought Kolchak's advance in the northern sector of the eastern front to a standstill. Comrade Stalin also displayed great activity on the western and north-western fronts in the first half of 1919. Finally, he was the originator of the plan for the annihilation of Denikin on the southern front in the autumn of 1919."

This official history keeps silence concerning the part played by Stalin in the Polish Campaign of 1920, but makes the following remarks about Trotsky:

"The Party won its victories in the Civil War over the principal enemies of the Soviet under Lenin's leadership and *against* the advice contained in Trotsky's plans. We cannot deny Trotsky's part in the Civil War as a propagandist and as an executant of the Central Committee's decisions, *when he chose to execute them*, but his strategy and his whole policy were vitiated by many organic defects. Trotsky's deep-rooted disbelief in the fitness of the proletariat to lead the peasantry and the fitness of the Party to lead the Red Army is characteristic of his strategy and policy. It explains his introduction of exclusively formal discipline and of the methods of compulsion customary in bourgeois armies; in it we may also see the reason of his endeavours to keep the Party as far removed from the army as possible, his boundless confidence in the bourgeois specialists, and his low opinion of the Red Army in comparison with the White Guard Armies. All this reflects the psychology of the former Tsarist officers who obtained staff posts."

Karl Radek wrote in similar fashion on February 23, 1935, the seventeenth anniversary of the Red Army. He called Stalin "the leader of the proletarian army and the military genius of the Civil War," but said of

Trotsky that he was "the prototype of the petty bourgeois vacillating general who overloaded the front with former Tsarist staff officers, without regard either to their attitude to the Revolution or to their military capabilities, and tried to impress it with his impossible general staff uniforms. But Stalin never cared a brass farthing for officers' epaulettes."

Not only do the official histories written to-day deny Trotsky all his deserts as leader of the Red Army; they also refuse to admit his rôle as leader of the October Revolution in Petrograd. No less a personage than Joseph Stalin himself has written the following words in his pamphlet entitled, *On Trotskyism.*

"I must say that Trotsky did not and could not play any leading part in the October Revolution. As chairman of the Petrograd Soviet, he merely gave effect to the will of the Party as expressed in its decrees, which guided his every step. He played no particular part either in the Party or in the October Revolution, and indeed could not do so, for he was still a comparatively junior member of our Party in those October days."

A leading article which appeared in *Pravda* on November 6, 1918, in commemoration of the first anniversary of the October Revolution, throws a somewhat different light on Trotsky's activities during those days, for it states:

"All the work and practical organization of the rising was carried out under the immediate leadership of Trotsky, the chairman of the Petrograd Soviet. We can state with all certainty that we owe the garrison's prompt adherence to the Soviet cause and the skilful organization of the work of the Party's Revolutionary War Committee first and foremost to Comrade Trotsky."

The writer of this article was Joseph Stalin, who appended to it his full signature.

Larissa Reissner, the Bolshevist girl who fought in the ranks of the Red Guard in the October Revolution and then entered the Red Army as a private, took part in 1919 in the Civil War as a commissar attached to the staff of the Baltic Fleet, and won a world-wide reputation in later days by her descriptions of the Civil War, depicts Trotsky at the front in her book *October*.

The passage I quote deals with the critical days of the Czechoslovak Insurrection, when the Red Army, then only in process of formation, had yet to meet its baptism of fire. Its regiments were retreating in panic before the onslaught of the Czechoslovaks. Kazan was lost, and the remains of the routed Red Army mustered in Sviyazhsk.

"Trotsky arrived at Sviyazhsk on the third or fourth day after the fall of Kazan. His armoured train drew up at the little station, with the evident intention of making a long stay. All Trotsky's organizational genius was promptly manifested. He contrived to make effective rationing arrangements and brought further batteries and several regiments to Sviyazhsk, despite the obvious breakdown of the railways—in short, he did everything necessary to cope with the impending attack. Moreover, we must not forget the work which had to be done in 1918, when the general demobilization was still exercising its destructive effects, and the appearance of a well-equipped Red Army detachment in the Moscow streets caused so great sensation. Trotsky, in those days, was swimming against the stream, against the weariness of four years of war and against the flood-tide of revolution that overflowed the whole land, carrying away with it the wreckage of the old Tsarist discipline and engendering a fierce hatred of everything that recalled memories of officers' orders, barracks and military life.

"In spite of everything, the rations became obviously better; newspapers, overcoats and boots arrived. And there, in the place where the boots were being served out, we found a genuine, permanent army staff. The army took firm root there and thought no more of flight.

"Trotsky contrived to endow his new-born army with an iron backbone. He took up his abode in Sviyazhsk with the firm determination not to yield an inch of territory. He contrived to be a wise, adamantine, unruffled leader to this little handful of defenders."

While the Red Army was preparing to attack Kazan, a large formation of White Guard troops gained the rear of the Soviet lines by night and attacked the railway-station of Sviyazhsk.

"Then L. D. Trotsky mobilized the whole personnel of the train—the clerks, telegraphists, ambulance men and his own bodyguard—in short, every man who could hold a rifle. The staff offices were emptied in the twinkling of an eye; there was no more 'base' for anyone."

All these improvised forces were hurled at the White Guards, who were then approaching the station.

"The White Guards thought they were fighting a new, well-organized body of troops; they did not guess that all the opposition they had to encounter was a hastily assembled handful of fighters, behind whom there was nobody but Trotsky himself and Slavin, the commander of the 5th Red Army. That night Trotsky's train remained there without its engine, as usual, while not a single unit of the 5th Army, which was about to take the offensive and had advanced some considerable distance from Sviyazhsk, had its rest disturbed by a recall from the front to aid in the defence of the almost unprotected town. The army and flotilla knew nothing about the night attack until it was all over, and the White Guards had retreated in the firm conviction that they had encountered practically a whole division.

"The next day twenty-seven deserters who had taken refuge on the steamers were court-martialled and shot. They included several Communists.

"Anyone who has lived with the Red Army, who has been born with it and grown up with it in the fighting at Kazan, can confirm the fact that the iron spirit of this army would never have solidified, and that the close contact between the Party and the mass of soldiers and the equally close contact between the ranker and the officer in supreme command would never have come into existence, if on the eve of the storming of Kazan, which was to cost the lives of so many hundreds of soldiers, the Party had not made this demonstration before the eyes of the whole army of men ready to make the supreme sacrifice for the Revolution, if it had not shown them that the rough laws of fraternal discipline were binding on its own members too, and that it had the courage to apply the laws of the Soviet Republic as ruthlessly to them as to other offenders.

"The twenty-seven were shot, and their corpses filled the breach that the Whites had made in the self-reliance and resolution of the 5th Army.

"An army of workers and peasants had to express itself in some way or other; it had to create its own outward aspect and take its own shape, but no one could prophesy in what manner it would accomplish this task. At that time there was naturally no dogmatic programme and no recipe for the growth and development of this mighty organism.

"There was only a premonition in the Party and the masses—a kind of creative conjecture concerning the nature of this hitherto unknown revolutionary military organization which obtained new and genuine characteristics from every day's fighting. Trotsky's special merit may be found in the fact that he needed only an instant to sense the slightest reaction in the masses of men who already bore the stamp of this unique organizational formula on their persons.

"Trotsky collected and systematized every little working method that could help besieged Sviyazhsk to simplify, arrange and speed up the war work.

"A man who is an excellent orator, and who has evolved the rational, flawless, plastic form of a new army may nevertheless freeze its spirit or let it dissipate. Such risks can only be eliminated if the man is also a great revolutionary with the creative intuition and hundred-kilowatt-strong inward wireless set, without which no one can approach the masses."

This initiative faculty Trotsky possessed.

"The soldier, commander and war commissar within him were never able to oust the revolutionary. And when in his superhuman metallic voice he denounced a deserter, he really feared in him the mutineer whose treachery or mean cowardice was so harmful and destructive, not merely to military operations but to the whole proletarian revolutionary cause."

These are the words of Larissa Reissner. We may add that Trotsky's great revolutionary ethics enabled him to visualize in the Red Army warriors not only his soldiers of the Civil War but also the builders of the future socialist order of society. When Wrangel's 'volunteers' sang in 1919:

> "A steamer is at hand,
> Against its sides the waves do beat,
> When the Red Army men try to land,
> We'll give them all to the fish to eat,"

the Red Army adapted it for their own purposes by
substituting:

"When Wrangel's volunteers try to land,
    We'll give them all to the fish to eat."

But Trotsky issued an army order forbidding this
parody, on the ground that Wrangel's volunteers were
merely men who had been led astray, and that the
Proletarian Revolution would find the way to bring
them over on to its own side. Such verses, he explained,
were merely the products of military brutalization,
which the soldiers of the Red Army must shun, because
they were the human material with which the Socialist
State was to be built up.

One of Trotsky's great merits as a Red Army
organizer was the way in which he applied his theoretical knowledge to the petty practical daily work of
building up the army. Shortly after the beginning of the
four years of civil war a group of Bolshevist military
workers propounded a 'Special Military Doctrine of the
Revolutionary Proletariat,' which culminated in a
'Theory of Total Offensive,' whereupon Trotsky gave
them the following reply:

"We must now devote our whole attention to improv-
ing our material and making it more efficient rather
than to fantastic schemes of re-organization. Every
army unit must receive its rations regularly, foodstuffs
must not be allowed to rot, and meals must be cooked
properly. We must teach our soldiers personal clean-
liness and see that they exterminate vermin. They must

learn their drill properly and perform it in the open air
as much as possible. They must be taught to make their
political speeches short and sensible, to clean their
rifles and grease their boots. They must learn to shoot,
and must help their officers to ensure strict observance
of the regulations for keeping in touch with other units
in the field, reconnaissance work, reports and sentry
duty. They must learn and teach the art of adaptation
to local conditions, they must learn to wind their
puttees properly so as to prevent sores on their legs,
and once again they must learn to grease their boots.
That is our programme for next year in general and
next spring in particular, and if anyone wants to take
advantage of any solemn occasion to describe this practical programme as 'military doctrine,' he's welcome to
do so."

With this definition of the tasks before it, Trotsky
gave the Red Army the lever it then needed to raise the
general standard of its efficiency.

Since we have already quoted Radek's 1935 opinion
of the part played by Trotsky in the evolution of the
Red Army, it would not be amiss to make further
quotations from the article entitled *Leo Trotsky,
Organizer of Victory*, which he wrote in 1923:

"Our State machinery is creaking and rumbling. But
our real great success is the Red Army. Its creator and
will-centre is Comrade L. D. Trotsky. The history of
the Proletarian Revolution has proved that pens ('Pen'
was Trotsky's pseudonym before the Revolution) can

be turned into swords. Trotsky is one of the best of writers on international socialism, but his literary gifts have not prevented him from becoming the first leader and the first organizer of the proletariat's first army.

"Trotsky's organizational genius was expressed in the courageous attitude he adopted to the idea of employing military specialists to build up the army. Only Trotsky's fiery faith in our social power, his faith in our ability to realize the best means of deriving profit from the knowledge of these military experts while refusing to allow them to dictate to us in political matters, his faith in the power of the vigilance of progressive workers to triumph over the counter-revolutionary intrigues of former Tsarist officers could break down the suspicions of our military workers and teach them to use the abilities of these officers. We could only find a successful practical solution of this problem by discovering an army chief with a will of iron who would not merely enjoy the Party's complete confidence but could also use his iron will to dominate the foremen whom he compelled to serve our cause. Not only did Comrade Trotsky find a way to subjugate these former officers of the old army to his will by virtue of the energy he displayed; he went still further, for he contrived to win the confidence of the best elements among the experts and convert them from enemies of Soviet Russia into convinced adherents of our cause.

"In this case the Russian Revolution has worked through the brain, heart and nerve system of its great representative. When we ventured upon the ordeal of battle for the first time, the Party and L. D. Trotsky showed us how to apply the principles of a political campaign to the conflict of arms in which we had to use arguments of steel. We concentrated all our material forces on war. Our whole party understands the necessity of doing so, but this necessity found its greatest expression in the steel determination of Trotsky.

"After our victory over Denikin in March 1920, Trotsky said to the Party Congress: 'We plundered all Russia in order to conquer the Whites!' In these few words he expressed the whole vast concentration of will which we needed for victory. We needed a man who could incarnate our call to battle, who could become a tocsin which summoned us to arms and to obedience to that will which demanded first and foremost unconditional subordination to the great and terrible necessity of war. Only a man who worked as Trotsky did, only a man who knew how to speak to soldiers as Trotsky spoke to them, only such a man could become the standard-bearer of armed workers.

"He was everything in one single person. He weighed the strategical advice of his experts in his brain and found the way to apply it to the greatest advantage under the social conditions as he saw them. He knew how to combine the impulses emanating from fourteen fronts and ten thousand Communists which told him at the centre what he might expect from the army, how best to work with it and what form to give it; he knew how to weld all these things into a strategical plan and an organizational scheme. And with all this magnificent work that he accomplished, he understood, as no one else did, the way to apply his knowledge of the significance of moral factors in war.

"Our army was a peasant army. In it the dictatorship of the proletariat, i.e., the command of this army by workers and representatives of the working classes, was brought about in the persons of Trotsky and the comrades who co-operated with him. It was accomplished, above all, by the way in which Trotsky drew upon the help of our whole Party machinery to inspire this war-weary army of peasants with the profound conviction that they were fighting for their own interests.

"Trotsky worked with our whole Party at the task of creating a Red Army. He could not have carried out this task without the Party's co-operation. But the creation of the Red Army and its victories would have demanded far greater sacrifices if he had not been there. If our Party is to be the first Party of the Proletariat which has succeeded in building up a great army, this glorious page in the history of the Russian Revolution must be coupled for ever with the name of Leo Davidovitch Trotsky, the man whose work and deeds will be matters not only of love, but also of study for the future generations of workers who set about the conquest of the whole world."

This was the judgement passed by Karl Radek on Trotsky's rôle as creator, organizer and leader of the

Red Army in February 1923, when Lenin still lived and he was under Lenin's control.

In his reminiscences of Lenin (*Vladimir Lenin*) Maxim Gorky has related a conversation he had with him. When in the course of it he mentioned the hostility shown by certain Bolshevists to Trotsky, Lenin banged his fist upon the table and said:

"Show me another man who could have practically created a model army in a year and won the respect of the military specialists as well. We have got such a man! We have got everything!"

Chapter Six

*Trotsky's Fall; Frunse
and Voroshilov*

In the autumn of 1924, a few months after Lenin's death, Zinoviev demanded Trotsky's removal from the post of War Commissar and his expulsion from the Party.

In the preface to his book on the October Revolution Trotsky passes a scathing criticism on Zinoviev's vacillating attitude in those days and on his opposition to the Party's decision to start the Revolution. Trotsky also puts the question: What would have happened if Zinoviev had been leader of the Party in 1917, if he had occupied the position of authority which was his in 1923 and again in 1924, when he was at the head of the Comintern?

The political deduction to be drawn from Trotsky's reasoning is that it would have been necessary to obtain leadership which offered the greatest personal guarantee against defeats similar to those suffered by the German proletariat in 1923 when circumstances were favourable to them.

In the autumn of 1924 the leadership of both Party

and State was vested in the so-called *Troika*[1] or trium-
virate of Zinoviev, Kamenev and Stalin. The last-
named, who had previously incited Zinoviev to sharp
action against Trotsky, suddenly appeared in the rôle
of 'mediator,' and so a compromise was arranged.
Trotsky was relieved of his military offices, but remained
a member of the Bolshevist Party.

Several months previously Sklansky, the first Deputy
War Commissar and Trotsky's closest confidential
friend, had been removed from office overnight while
on leave and sent to America, where he was destined to
be drowned a year later on a motor-boat trip. His place
was filled by Michael Frunse, an intimate friend of
Zinoviev. The relations of Trotsky and Frunse in the
War Commissariat were in the nature of mutual antagonism rather than co-operation.

Frunse was an old Bolshevist, of the professional
revolutionary type. He was an army surgeon's son,
born at Pishpek, in Central Asia, in 1885; after passing
his Secondary School Matriculation, he studied econo-
mics at the Petersburg Technical School, but was sent
down in 1904 for participating in a Marxist course.

In the following year we find him active as an
organizer of the Bolshevist Party at Ivanovo-Vozne-
sensk, the centre of the Russian textile industry. He
was a delegate to the 3rd Party Day (London 1905) and
the 4th Party Day (Stockholm, 1906), but in the follow-

---

[1] A Russian team of three horses driven abreast. (Translator's
Note.)

ing year he was arrested and sentenced to four years'
imprisonment. A year later he was sentenced to death
for 'resisting the State authority,' but the Court of
Appeal commuted the sentence to six years' penal
servitude.

Frunse escaped from prison at Chita in 1915. At the
time of the February Revolution of 1917 he was carrying on illegal military work at Minsk; later on he
became leader of the Bolshevist Party for White Russia
and on the western front. In October 1917, he came to
Moscow at the head of 2,000 armed workmen. He
became Military Commissar at Yaroslavl in the summer
of 1918, an army commander on the eastern front in
December of the same year, and was appointed to lead
a group of armies on this front in 1919. The forces
under him defeated Kolchak and won Turkestan for the
Soviets. He also directed the final operations against
Wrangel in the Crimea, where he displayed great
personal courage at the storming of Perekop.

Frunse was a highly educated man, who combined a
great talent for organization with painstaking thorough-
ness. He held his post as War Commissar only for a
few months; then he died in consequence of an operation for gall-stones, which was forced upon him against
his will by the Central Committee. The medical board
which examined him did not pronounce in favour of
the operation, but stated that he would never be completely fit for work without it. Thereupon Stalin
induced the Party to order him to undergo it.

The choice of Frunse's successor caused a conflict within the *Troika*. First Zinoviev proposed Lashevitch, an old Bolshevist who took a prominent part in military work during the Civil War; this was the man who promoted an illegal meeting of the Zinoviev opposition group in a wood near Moscow some years later, for which offence he was relieved of his post and exiled to Siberia, where he died.

Stalin's candidate was Ordyonikidse. When Zinoviev realized his inability to secure the post for Lashevitch, he made a daring attempt to eliminate Stalin from the leadership of both Party and State by proposing him as War Commissar. Later on Stalin admitted to friends that this proposal came as a revelation to him and made him realize that the differences between Zinoviev and himself must inevitably lead to a struggle for power, in which one or the other would have to go under.

At last their comedy of intrigue ended with a compromise which gave Voroshilov a temporary appointment as Frunse's successor. Zinoviev was convinced he would find no great difficulty in winning this man over to his political views, for he was easily influenced and not particularly intelligent. But Zinoviev was destined to have an unfortunate experience with Voroshilov.

It came when the two men were on leave together in the Crimea. There Zinoviev divulged his plans to Voroshilov, and thought he had convinced the new War Commissar of the necessity of breaking Stalin's exces-

sive influence. Voroshilov promised to support him:
he then attended a meeting of the Central Committee,
where he came out with revelations of Zinoviev's
designs that hastened the latter's fall.

Voroshilov has a hard proletarian life behind him.
He is a railway-worker's son, born in 1881; at the age
of seven he was put to work, and so could not go to
school. At first he worked underground in the mines;
later on, he became a farm labourer under a *kulak*.
After that he worked as a shepherd, but at the age of
twelve he had the chance to attend a village school. At
fifteen he was employed in a metal works, and at
seventeen underwent his first arrest when he was taken
into custody for participation in a strike.

When employed as a metal worker in the Hartmann
factory in Lugansk in 1903, he made his first contact
with Marxist circles. In 1906 the young workman was
a delegate to the Stockholm Party Day; the following
year he was arrested for illegal work, but escaped shortly
afterwards and went to Baku on Party business. From
that time onward he was in touch with Stalin.

At the outbreak of the World War he was living in
exile, but was influenced by Chauvinist propaganda to
volunteer for active service. During the February
Revolution he found his way back to the Party
fold.

Voroshilov has never been able to fill the gaps in his
education, although he made earnest endeavours to do
so, at least during his first few years at the War Com-

missariat. His authority in the Higher Command of the
Red Army was and is slight, for he has always been
regarded as a mere mouthpiece of the Bolshevist Party
leaders. He has never developed any independent
military ideas in the sessions of the Revolutionary
Council of War, although he has displayed a certain
originality in designing new uniforms for various military units. He was responsible for the re-introduction
of all the old officer ranks, from lieutenant to field-
marshal, in 1936.

Voroshilov entered upon his new post with two
Orders of the Red Flag which he had won in the Civil
War. As soon as he was in office, he awarded himself
two more for gallant deeds performed at that period—
an unnecessary gesture, for his courage was well known
throughout the whole army.

Trotsky sums him up as follows in an article dated
June 17, 1937:

"It is no secret that the old Bolshevist Voroshilov
is a purely decorative figure. In Lenin's lifetime no one
would have dreamed of electing him to the Central
Committee. Although his personal courage in the Civil
War is undeniable, he displayed a complete lack of
military and administrative abilities and showed the
outlook of a backwoodsman. Neither Stalin nor any
other member of the Politburo had any illusions about
his qualities as a military leader, and for that reason
they made efforts to support him in office by giving
him the assistance of expert colleagues."

With these words Trotsky has voiced the opinions current in the Higher Officers' Corps as well as among the heads of the Party and government.

Nevertheless the 'First Red Marshal of the Soviet Union' is a popular figure in the eyes of. the younger generation and the privates of the Red Army. Voroshilov is an excellent rider and a superb shot who takes part in many shooting competitions inside and outside the army. It is the ideal of every Red soldier and every young Soviet citizen to become a 'Voroshilov shot,' i.e., to shoot as well as Voroshilov and receive a badge for his prowess.

The real leaders of the Red Army during the last few years have been Tuchachevsky and Gamarnik. Their best immediate subordinates were the three members of the Soviet Union Council of War and commanders of the most important military districts—Yakir, Uborevitch and Blücher.

Army Organization.

The first definite pronouncement on the structure of the new army is to be found in the *Ten Theses of Soviet Power*, which Lenin drew up for the 7th Party Day in March 1918,[1] Section 5 prescribes:

"The creation of armed forces of peasants and workers who must remain in as close contact as possible with the people (the Soviets and the armed peasants

[1] See Appendix I.

and workers). The organization of a general arming of
the people as the first step towards a whole nation in
arms."

This resolution was adopted in concrete form in the
Party programme drawn up for the 8th Party Day in
March 1919.[1] It provided for a complete introduction
of the militia system, on the ground that "in contra-
distinction to the structure of the old army, it is necessary to make the period of instruction in barracks as
brief as possible. The barracks must approximate to a
military-political school and secure the closest possible
contact between the military formations and the factories, works, trade unions and organizations of the
poorer villagers."

The Civil War prevented the Soviet Government from
attempting to realize this programme in 1919. In April
1920, shortly before the outbreak of the Russo-Polish
War, the 9th Party Day decided, in a special resolution,
entitled, "The Transition to the Militia System," to
build up a Red Peace Army on the general principles
of the militia system. This resolution stated, however,
that "the workers' and peasants' militias must be based
on cadres that have received military technical and
political preparation."[1]

After the Russo-Polish War the future form of the
army became the subject of violent discussions in the
Party, and even more violent ones in the ranks of the
officers. The supporters of the militia system and the

[1] See Appendix I.

advocates of a standing army represented two extremely antagonistic points of view, the chief spokesman for the latter system being Tuchachevsky, who published in January 1921, a polemic entitled *The Red Army and the Militia,* in which he expressed his own standpoint most pungently. It is interesting to note the daring trends of thought of this officer who commanded an army at the age of twenty-eight, though it must be admitted that he sometimes expresses them with too much acerbity:

"The adherents of the militia system take absolutely no account of Soviet Russia's present military mission of disseminating socialist revolution throughout the world. The rich varieties of socialist life and the socialist revolution cannot be forced into any particular framework. They will spread irresistibly over the whole world, and their expanding force will endure so long as there is a bourgeoisie left anywhere.

"What is the way in which they will best achieve their aims? It is the way of armed insurrection within every state, or the way of armed socialist attacks on bourgeois states, or a combination of both ways. No one can make definite prophecies, for the course of the Revolution will show us the right way. One thing, however, is certain: if a socialist revolution succeeds in gaining power in any country, it will have a self-evident right to expand, and will strive to cover the whole world by making its immediate influence felt in all neighbouring countries. Its most powerful instrument will naturally be its military forces.

"The structure of an army is determined on the one hand by the political aims it pursues and on the other by the recruiting system it employs. It is self-evident that a proletariat which has emerged victorious from a class war cannot recruit its army by the ordinary form of national compulsory military service. The obligation to serve in it must affect the working classes alone.

"We therefore see that the Socialist Revolution has created a new recruiting system for its international class army, thus forming a contrast to the bourgeois revolutions which evolved national and democratic armies.

"The characteristic features of a militia army are its vast size and its comparatively small war efficiency. Large armies which lack the nuclei of permanent military formations can receive no thorough training with regular units in time of peace, since they are assembled only by mobilization orders. Their war efficiency is therefore bound to be small.

"This defect must be remedied in some way or other, and the most suitable way is by the method of war technique. The success of a militia system is dependent on an extremely well constructed network of communications which permits of the transport of men by railway, motor vehicle and waterway. It can become a source of great strength—but only when the State in question has practically all its land under cultivation and possesses great wealth and highly developed industries. A militia army is not worth a brass farthing if it lacks these vast reserves of man-power and a military technique which can be applied to the utmost limits. In our case the introduction of the militia system would be tantamount to a crucifixion of Soviet Russia."

Tuchachevsky considered the militia system "an antiquated idea, or, more correctly, an antiquated superstition dating from the period of the Second International," which was not inspired by the principle of a socialist offensive. Lenin and Trotsky, and with them the majority of the Bolshevist Party, were, however, not at that time in agreement with Tuchachevsky's point of view.

Tuchachevsky envisaged the creation of a modern revolutionary army, ready and able to defend Soviet Russia against imperialist attacks and to assist the proletariats of other countries and the colonial races with armed fraternal aid in their struggles against their oppressors. But the internal conditions necessary for the creation of such an army were lacking, since the closer and better relations between the working classes and the peasantry which they presupposed did not yet exist. The Red Army had therefore to be built up in a way that would enable it to serve first and foremost as a link between town and country.

The years 1922 and 1923 were occupied with the difficult task of demobilizing the millions who served in the Civil War. In 1924 a beginning was made with the

construction of the Red Army on the general principles
laid down by the military programme of the 9th Party
Day.

From that time onward obligatory service in Russia
has been divided into three parts: (1) preliminary
training; (2) service with the colours; (3) service in the
reserve. Service with the colours is performed in either
the regular, standing, so-called 'Cadre Army,' or in
the 'Territorial Army,' which is based on the militia
system. The period of service in the regular army
varies according to the arm; in the infantry it is two
years, in the artillery and some other specialized
corps three years, and in the navy and air force four
years.

There was originally a regulation by which only men
of proletarian or semi-proletarian ancestry were eligible
for service in the army, by which sons of *kulaks*, priests,
or other persons who had not obtained full Soviet
citizenship were excluded. This restrictive regulation
was, however, abolished in 1937.

All men mustered for service had to pass three recruiting commissions. The first of these was the 'Social
Commission,' which had to ascertain whether the
recruit's social origin rendered him eligible for service
in the Red Army; this commission also divided the
recruits into groups according to their social dispen-
sibility, some sons of peasants working one-man farms
being assigned to the Territorial Army along with
youthful workmen and employees with relatives depen-

dent upon their earnings. Then came the 'Medical Commission,' which assigned the recruits to the following categories:

(1) Unfit for military service.
(2) Fit for service with the Territorial Army.
(3) Fit for service with the Cadre Army.
(4) Fit for service with the artillery, navy, air force, and special branches.

Finally, the 'Military Commission' assigned the recruits to the Territorial or Cadre Army and posted them to the arms in which they were to serve in one or other army system. Recruits serving with the tank corps, air force or navy had to pass certain examinations (psychotechnical and other) after a period of probation.

In the Territorial Army training was spread over a number of years, but on an average the territorial recruit could count on a five-year period, eight to eleven months of which would be passed with his unit. These included two months' service in barracks for the first year, followed by periods of about six weeks in camp or on manœuvres in subsequent years.

The territorial conscripts residing in a particular area formed a military unit of some particular territorial formation, which was commanded by reserve officers belonging to that district.

The system in force for mustering recruits living on the steppes is as follows: the eligible men from three villages are assembled, and thereupon constitute a unit of their regiment, although as yet unarmed. Under the charge of a few officers, they converge by foot marches, motor, rail and water transport on the regimental depot, and the regiment is deemed to be formed as soon as they have drawn their uniform and equipment.

In the event of mobilization these territorial formations have to co-operate in speeding up the marches of the regular Red Army.

The territorial system provides the minimum interruption of industrial and economic life by the performance of military service. Peasant territorials are only called up for training in the months in which they can be most easily spared from their work on the land. Workmen employed in factories receive their usual pay during their periods of service. In contrast to the Swiss militia system, Russian territorials do not take their uniform, arms and other equipment home with them on completion of their military training.

The disadvantage of this form of training is to be found in the inferior military value of the men who undergo it. According to Gussov, the experiences of the Civil War show that "territorial formations fight principally for their hearths and homes. They are loth to take part in offensives or retreats which remove them from the vicinity of their dwellings and families."

The organizational form of the Russian Cadre Army is similar to that which may be found in any imperialist standing army. But until 1934, 74 per cent of the Red Army's divisions were territorial ones, leaving only 26 per cent for the standing army. In 1935 these proportions were reversed, and we now have 77 per cent of the troops in regular divisions, and only 23 per cent in the territorial forces.

From 1923 to 1934 the strength of the Cadre Army was about 560,000 men. It was then increased to 940,000 in 1935 and finally in 1936 to 1,300,000, distributed among all branches of the defence forces. These figures do not include the men serving in the Red Territorial Army.

From 1935 onwards the regular divisions have been gradually brought up to war strength, and on January 1, 1936, Tuchachevsky stated in his report to the Central Executive Committee of the Soviets that "the training for war given in peace time approximates as closely as possible to the conditions of actual war service. Our system is as perfect as it can be for both mobilization and training purposes."

We may thus note that Tuchachevsky's original demands have not been fulfilled. But the political hypotheses on which he based them in 1921 no longer exist.

The Political Aspect of the Red Army.

The military oath taken by the men of the Red Army was in its first form as follows:

"In entering hereby into the community of the Red Army of workers and peasants, and taking upon myself deliberately and of my own free will the duty of giving aid in the hard and holy wars of the oppressed peoples, I swear to my brothers in arms, to the whole nation of workers and to my own revolutionary conscience that I am ready to fight worthily and without fear, treachery or misgiving for the great cause for which the children of the best families of workers and peasants have already given their lives, for the victory of the Soviet power and the triumph of socialism."

On taking over the War Commissariat, Trotsky devised a new form of military oath, which bound the soldiers of the Red Army to serve not merely Soviet Russia and the Russian workers, but the proletariat of the whole world:

"(1) I, son of working-class parents and a citizen of the Union of Socialist Soviet Republics, assume the title of a soldier in the Army of Workers and Peasants.

"(2) Before the workers of the Union of Socialist Soviet Republics and the whole world I pledge myself to bear this title in honour, to learn the art of war conscientiously and to cherish as the apple of my eye the property of the people and protect it against all robbery and destruction.

"(3) I pledge myself to observe revolutionary discipline strictly and resolutely and to obey without demur all orders given me by the commanders set over me by the government of workers and peasants.

"(4) I pledge myself to abstain from all actions derogatory to the dignity of a citizen of the Soviet Union and to restrain my comrades from such actions, and to direct my every action and thought towards the freeing of all workers.

"(5) I pledge myself to respond to the first call from the government of workers and peasants by placing myself at its disposal for the defence of the republic of workers and peasants against any attack and peril from any enemy, and to spare neither my strength nor my life in battle for the Union of Socialist Soviet Republics and for the cause of socialism and the fraternization of all races.

"(6) May the scorn of all be my lot and may the hard hand of the revolutionary law punish me, if ever with evil intent I break this my solemn oath."

The entire political educational work in the ranks of the Red Army was permeated at first by this spirit of internationalism. The magnitude of the mission it set itself becomes apparent when we realize that the peasants constituted far the greater part of the army. But, as Gussov wrote in 1921, "If the Tsar's barracks, schools and press were able to turn the peasants into soldiers capable of shooting down their fathers and brothers, why should not we accomplish the task of creating from those same peasants an army that would give assistance to the World Revolution?"

The leadership of the army was undertaken by the threefold authority of commander, commissar and political administrator. The military leadership devolved on the commander. The office of commissar was created in order to keep the commanders under political observation. Additional to these was the 'Political Administration' of the Army, which was a component part of the War Commissariat (later known as the Defence Commissariat); this was an institution of some importance, subject, however, to the immediate control of the Party. The first chief of the Political Administration was Gussov; his successor was Bubnov, who gave way in turn to Gamarnik, the last-named holding office until May 1937. All three were members of the Central Committee of the Communist Party of the Soviet Union.

The Political Administration worked through the instrumentality of the Party Cells, which existed in every unit from the general staff down to the companies. As long as Lenin's Party principles that "every member of the Party is responsible for the whole Party, and the Party is responsible for every individual," held good, these Party cells were able to deal with every political question arising within the army, and took a hand in shaping the Party policy on the basis of democratic centralism. Moreover, they exercised a political and moral control over both their own members and non-party officers and soldiers.

Finally, the Political Administration organized and directed the whole of the vast cultural and political educational work within the army by means of political instruction, political schools and courses, libraries and literature dissemination, wall and Red Army newspapers, theatres, cinemas, Lenin corners, contacts with the factories and villages, Red Aid Work, the Society for Air and Chemical Defence (*Ossoaviachim*), musical and dramatic societies, sports clubs, chess clubs, etc. Illiterate recruits were taught to read and write in the first few months of their training, while a large number of soldiers were prepared during their final year for future civilian employment in positions such as tractor-drivers, machine-minders, leaders of collective farms and specialized industrial workers; in many cases these men received instruction by means of courses lasting several weeks which they were detailed to attend at the factories. Thus the Red Army provided the villages with entire cadres of qualified organizers and workers.

In Party work there was no distinction between officers and privates; the only differences recognized were those between Party members, candidates and non-party men. A communist company-commander who behaved in an uncommunist way in service or private life had to answer for his conduct to the cell, the secretary of which might possibly be his direct military subordinate. If a non-party officer sought admission to the Party, he had to submit to an all-round searching examination of his

political and human qualities at a Party meeting, to
which the other non-Party men were admitted. In such
cases privates, who might even be natives of the same
village as their officer, came forward to report on his
past political tendencies and his personal behaviour to
his fellow-men and subordinates, and asked questions
to which he had to give detailed practical answers. The
decision as to his acceptance or rejection then rested
with the Party cell and Party authorities above it.

As long as democratic principles ruled in the Party,
these military cells constituted a valuable guarantee
for the continuance and intensification of the proletarian
class character of the Red Army. They formed a pro-
tective wall against the development of a definite officer
class.

The social and economic distinctions between all
ranks of the Red Army remained extremely slight during
the first few years of peace. The Red officers—especially
those who belonged to the Communist Party—were
restricted to an extremely Spartan mode of life.

I can recall an incident which took place in 1925, just
after motor-buses made their first appearance in the
Moscow streets. When leaving barracks, I asked the
company-commander, who happened to be with me, to
accompany me on a bus to the centre of the town. He
refused in all seriousness, on the ground that it was
not fitting for a proletarian commander to ride in a
'motor.'

In 1924 the pay of a corps-commander was 150

roubles a month, corresponding roughly to that earned by a well-paid metal worker. It was thus 25 roubles a month below the 'Party maximum,' i.e. the largest monthly salary that a Party member was allowed to accept in those days. The commander of a division received 100 roubles a month, and a company-commander 43 roubles. A group-leader (non-commissioned officer) received only 15 roubles a month.

There was at that time no special officers' mess. The meals of officers and men were prepared in the same kitchens. Communist officers seldom wore the badges of their rank when off duty, and frequently dispensed with them even when on duty. At that time the Red Army acknowledged a relationship of superior and subordinate only during the performance of military duty, and in any case every soldier knew his commanding officer with or without badges of rank.

Officers' servants were abolished. The officers had therefore to clean their own boots. I remember another incident in 1925, which took place at a summer camp in the Volga district. While the troops were on duty, a private, who happened to be a peasant from the German Volga settlements, was sent to his company-commander's tent to fetch a map. Happening to notice that his commanding officer's boots were dirty, he sat down outside the tent and began to clean them. The consequence of his action was a complaint against both the officer in question and the secretary of the company's Party cell.

The officer was able to prove himself innocent of this 'relapse into Tsarist abuses,' but the cell secretary was reprimanded for failing to give the soldier sufficient instruction in proletarian class-consciousness. Thereafter the regimental dramatic society produced a number of scenes of barrack-room life in Tsarist days, in which officers' servants and boot-polishing were the principal themes.

The 'basic mission' of the political educational work was, as Gussov wrote in 1921 when head of the Political Administration, "to turn a large proportion of the peasants into international communists and the rest— or, at least, the younger generation—into sympathetic supporters of the idea of a revolutionary war of aggression, because the idea of a revolutionary war of defence was one which the peasant could grasp comparatively easily." Gussov also gave the following practical hints for the performance of this international educational work:

"Education in the spirit of internationalism naturally presupposes in the first place that the Red Army man will be familiar with the A.B.C. of communism. Without this theoretical basis we can make no progress. The crux of the matter is not, however, to be found in an abstract internationalism, but in the daily initiation of the soldier into the sphere of interest of the World Revolution by way of his immediate peasant interests. Otherwise the work will be useless.

"For example, the instructor must be able to link the

fate of a peasant's land in the Ufa district with the fate
of the World Revolution, and prove beyond all possibility of argument that only the success of the World
Revolution can sanction that peasant's permanent right
to his land. From the peasant's land in the Ufa district
to the World Revolution may be a very long way, but
it must none the less be traversed by showing the
peasant where his real interests lie. We have prepared
concrete instruction material of this type in the form of
instances of the help given us and our peasantry by the
proletariat of Western Europe during the Civil War and
once again during the famine. It is only a step from
these instances to the idea of mutual assistance and to
conceptions of the Russian peasantry's duty towards
the World Revolution."

The work of education was supplemented by addresses
from delegates belonging to the Communist Parties of
other countries, political emigrants (Red Aid), and
representatives of the colonial peoples.

The Red Army literature was also devoted to the task
of awakening and intensifying the internationalism of
the soldiers. In 1929 a revolutionary play entitled *The
First Red Cavalry Army* was produced in the Red
Army's Central House in Moscow. The cast was made
up entirely of amateurs belonging to the Red Army, the
female parts being played by officers' wives. In one
scene a Russian soldier was condemned to be 'shot by
the enemy' for revolutionary propaganda during the
World War, i.e., at the command of his lieutenant he

was forced by non-commissioned officers with loaded
revolvers to climb on to the breastwork of the trench
and expose himself to the German bullets. Amid the
excitement and indignation of his comrades, who nevertheless dared not mutiny, he climbed up, but instead of
the death-dealing bullets expected from the enemy
trenches there came only a shout in German:
"Comrades, we won't shoot!" Thereupon the
German proletarian soldiers came up out of their
trenches and fraternized with their Russian class comrades.

Several foreign communists who witnessed this play
with me spoke to Gamarnik in the interval and told
him of the ineradicable impression made on them by
such an internationalist paean expressed in the form of
dramatic art. Gamarnik took us behind the scenes
and introduced us to the actors playing the leading
parts of the 'Tsarist Lieutenant' and the 'soldier.' We
discovered that the stage 'soldier' was a lieutenant
belonging to a company of the 1st Proletarian Rifle
Regiment, while the 'lieutenant' who cursed and struck
him and afterwards ordered him to the breastwork was
a private in his platoon, i.e., an immediate subordinate
of the 'soldier' he maltreated on the stage. "Could any
imperialist army do a thing like that without undermining the whole basis of military discipline?" asked
Gamarnik with a smile.

In 1924 I wrote a play for the Red Army at Gamarnik's request. Its subject was the war on capitalism

waged by the Bavarian Red Army, whose ranks contained a number of Russian and Italian prisoners of war,
who were willing to give their lives for the German and
International Revolution.

In 1929 a young Red Army soldier of peasant origin
tried to explain the basis of socialist discipline to a
German Reichswehr general, who paid a visit to the
Central House. In one of the club-rooms the general
found a class of officers and men sitting together on
school benches to receive instruction in the German
language.

He asked a Red divisional-commander who was taking part in the class how this state of affairs could be
reconciled with military discipline. It might happen, he
pointed out, that the instructress put a question to the
officer which he could not answer. If one of his soldiers
answered it, he would be made to look a fool in front
of his men.

"On the contrary, we vie with one another in
socialistic emulation," replied the divisional-commander
with a smile.

"And why shouldn't I learn German better than the
Comrade divisional-commander?" asked a private
sitting next to the general. "He's a great authority for
me, because he's my instructor in military and political
affairs, and about these I can learn a lot from him. But
in everything else, in all agricultural matters, for
instance, I am a great authority for him. We peasants
were detailed for harvest work after the last autumn

manœuvres, and then I led a squad of twenty-four men, because I am an experienced farmer. The commander of my own regiment was working under me; he's a metal-worker and knows nothing about farming. He'd have made a proper fool of himself if he'd had to run our squad on harvest work."

The international spirit and socialistic basis of discipline in the Red Army were swept away during the years 1931–3, which were a time of severe crisis. Nowadays the entire educational work is concentrated on inculcating a 'Soviet Union patriotism' and nationalistic arrogance. The consequence of the policy of bloc alliances with imperialist governments was that the conception of class struggles within the imperialist states and struggles of oppressed colonial races against imperialist states had to give way to the opposite theory of 'friendly' and 'hostile' states and their citizens. The effect of this is that to-day a Red Army man—or, indeed, any average Soviet citizen—regards a German as his 'enemy' and a Frenchman or American (even if it be Mr. Pierpont Morgan himself) as his 'friend.'

The natural and easy relations between officers and men in the Red Army have also gone by the board. The Red officers now form a closed, privileged caste. Certain democratic army institutions were abolished soon after Voroshilov took office. Even as far back as 1926 officers' pay underwent large increases. Officers' messes were re-established; the ordinary military relationships between officers and men both on and off duty were reintroduced at the same time. In numerous cases the 'rise in the cultural level' of officers caused them to obtain divorces from wives of proletarian or peasant origin, who were not up to 'Society' standards, and to marry women belonging to the circles of the old aristocracy, the former bourgeoisie or the new bureaucracy. This was, in fact, a mass phenomenon.

The Soviet officer's standard of life is now no lower than that of his colleagues in imperialist armies, but the standard of life of the mass of the people and of the privates in the Red Army still falls considerably below the corresponding standards in Western Europe and America. Like the 'commanders' of the Stalinist bureaucracy, the officers of the Red Army now form a special privileged class which has cut adrift from the mass of Soviet Union workers and risen high above it. A special type of 'non-political' officer has been created. The senior officers who were drawn from the old Tsarist officer class remained essentially alien to proletarian internationalism, while the junior ones, even when of proletarian origin, began to hate internationalism as a disturbing element. They are happy to live their 'life of comfort,' and consequently they sing the *Internationale* or utter the form of oath devised for the Red Army by Trotsky as mechanically as any average Christian repeats his catechism.

These 'non-political' officers regard the policy of bloc alliances inaugurated by Stalin and Litvinov as a guarantee for the permanency and strengthening of their privileged position. Their champion in the army is now Voroshilov, the old advocate of guerilla warfare who once proclaimed a crusade against the 'wearers of epaulettes,' military discipline and the system of a centralized army. But, after all, it was Voroshilov who once maintained that the essential difference between a proletarian and an imperialist army was to be found in their varying forms of organization instead of in the different ideology and politics that dictated the aims and objects for which they were created. Over-valuation of outward forms has always been one of his prominent characteristics.

The Red Army does not merely exist on paper; it is now a live component part of the body of the Soviet Union. But its political aspect has undergone the same change as the political aspect of the whole Soviet Union has undergone under the autocratic Stalinist régime.

M. N. Tuchachevsky

Immediately after Voroshilov's assumption of office in 1925 Tuchachevsky was removed from his key position on the staff of the Red Army. He was sent first to Leningrad as commander of a military district, and later to Minsk.

At that time a commission set up by Trotsky and presided over by Tuchachevsky was still working on the new field service regulations for the Red Army. Its members, including Yakir, Uborevitch, Primakov, and Eydeman, protested their inability to dispense with his valuable co-operation, and so the man exiled to the provinces remained president of the body which established the first tactical and strategical foundations of the Red Army in these field-service regulations.

In his preface to the *Provisional Regulations for Field Service*, which appeared in the winter of 1925–6 Tuchachevsky launched a sharp attack on the theory which found its principal advocate in Voroshilov, who maintained that "the Red Army cannot undertake the task of rising to the technical standard of imperialist armies; it must win victories by its enthusiasm." Tuchachevsky called such conceptions "foolish chatter which helps the counter-revolution" and put forward the view that "the superior technique of imperialist armies must be overcome by the Red Army's evolution and mastery of a still more powerful technique."

Tuchachevsky served in the provinces for more than five years, but remained all the time the army's spiritual chief. He continued to give instruction at the War Academy, and his articles on organizational, tactical and strategic problems still appeared in military technical journals. All efforts to induce him to publish some condemnation of Trotsky which might smooth his path to advancement in the Red Army broke down on account of his upright character and his fanatical devotion to the truth.

But meanwhile the aspect of foreign affairs had undergone a change. In the Far East the petty warfare on the Manchurian frontier threatened to develop into warlike operations on a large scale. Consequently there was a movement among the leaders of the Red Army to bring Tuchachevsky back to the General Staff. Voroshilov's resistance was broken down, and Tuchachevsky was appointed chief of the Operations Department of the Red Army. He had been out of the Soviet public eye for years, and it was only when the victory of Fascism in Germany rendered the danger of war on two fronts acute that the Central Committee came to the decision to boost his popularity throughout the land. They were aware that the Commander-in-Chief in the coming war would have to be well known to the mass of the people, and so from that time onward Tuchachevsky took Voroshilov's place as the principal speaker on home defence at all the Soviet Congresses.

He directed his main efforts to overcoming the technical and tactical unprogressiveness which was a legacy of Tsarism. The principal problem was the mechanization of the Red Army.

The original champion and propagandist of mechanization was Trotsky. In 1924 he had introduced the subject of the motorization and mechanization of the Red Army at a mass meeting on the October Field in Moscow with the words: "Give the Red Army its motors!"

In his demand for mechanization Tuchachevsky was

supported by Feldmann. This Odessa Bolshevist, from whom the Boulevard Feldmann in his native town takes its name, was then in charge of the War Department of the People's Commissariat for Heavy Industries, and worked in close contact with his deputy, People's Commissar Piatakov.

Tuchachevsky likewise paid particular attention to the Air Force. For some years he had studied the problem of combining the functions of aeroplane and tank in a machine to be known as the 'flying tank,' i.e., an armoured car which automatically or by a few turns of a handle could be transformed into an aeroplane and then changed back again into a tank that was ready to go into action as soon as it landed. There is also a compromise solution of this problem in the form of large-sized aircraft which can transport a tank by air and land it behind the enemy's lines.

The study of the 'flying tank' led to successful experiments in the large-scale employment of special shock troops that could be dropped behind the enemy's lines by parachute. It is no mere chance that this idea of aerial infantry originated in the brain of Tuchachevsky, the Commander-in-Chief of the first Red Army of workers and peasants.

The idea of dropping such detachments in the enemy's rear presupposes that this area is peopled by inhabitants in sympathy with the aerial invaders, for otherwise such aerial shock troops as survived the attentions of the enemy's anti-aircraft batteries would be wiped out by mechanized units hastily despatched to deal with them. The conception of a parachute corps is therefore closely connected with the idea of an international Socialist Revolution. In 1921, when Tuchachevsky was still in a position to make open propaganda for his theories of internationalism, he wrote as follows:

"The socialist revolution has revolutionized a strategy. Our Red Army will never fight an adversary unaided, for it will always find the support it expects from the workers of the country with whose bourgeoisie it is at war. This support will not be confined to revolutionary outbreaks in the rear of the enemy's armies, since one of its essential points is the fact that reinforcements can be recruited from the workers inhabiting the territory occupied by the Red Army. Such reinforcements will not merely be drawn from the local population; they will also come from the man-power of capitalist armies. This accession of a stream of international fighting forces is a characteristic feature of the Red Army methods of warfare."

Ten years later he was not in a position openly to propagate his ideas as to the international nature of the Red Army, but he acted upon them by creating the preliminary technical conditions for giving support to socialist revolutions in other countries. The parachute detachments were to become the helpers of the proletarians, in any imperialist country that were fighting for their freedom. He also made a thorough study of the problems attendant on the landing of aerial infantry in the Ruhr, in East Prussia and in the territory between Berlin and Saxony, so that they might hasten to the assistance of the German proletariat in the event of revolution. Thus military history will couple the evolution of aerial infantry with the name of Tuchachevsky.

The cadre problem was still a sore point in the Red Army. The old officers who had made their careers in the Tsarist Army or in the Civil War were still too steeped in the traditions of an army that did not derive its power and rapidity of action from mechanized or motorized infantry. At the 17th Party Day of the Communist Party of the Soviet Union in 1934, Voroshilov said:

"There was a time when all of us—Comrade Yakir, Comrade Tuchachevsky, Comrade Uborevitch and all the other members of the Higher Command and Revolutionary Council of War—were troubled by the question: Will the officers and men of our Red Army be able to master the new technique, of which they are still ignorant?" Voroshilov then named as the Red Army's chief instructors the three men whom he and Stalin were three years later to send to execution. If the Red officers and men have made some progress towards the mastery of the new technique, it is mainly due to the efforts of this trio that they have done so.

Under Tuchachevsky's direction new curricula were drawn up for the War Academy and the Higher and

Lower Commands, and new methods of instruction worked out. But his own sole special subject was strategy, and the special mission for which he prepared himself was the command of Russia's forces in the event of hostilities between the Soviet Union and some imperialist power.

Was he really the great general that his co-operators, the Central Committee of the Bolshevist Party and the whole Soviet Union once deemed him to be?

Marshal Pilsudski, the greatest military adversary against whom Tuchachevsky pitted his strength in a major war, wrote as follows:

"Tuchachevsky inspired his subordinates by virtue of his energetic and purposeful work. This fine quality of leadership stamps him for ever as a general with daring ideas and the gift of putting them into vigorous execution. He gives me the impression of a general who tends to abstract ideas, but displays will-power, energy and a strange obstinacy in the working methods he has chosen for himself. Generals of this type are seldom capable of taking a broad view, because they link, so to speak, their whole personalities exclusively with their immediate tasks; on the other hand, they give the assurance that they will show no hesitation in carrying out the work they undertake. Tuchachevsky handled his troops very skilfully, and anyone can easily discern the signs of a general of the first order in his daring but logically correct march on Warsaw."

This is Pilsudski's opinion of Tuchachevsky at the

age of twenty-seven. A contemporary judgement passed on Napoleon when he undertook his Egyptian Campaign at a similar age would hardly have been different.

The final judgement passed on Tuchachevsky by his immediate chief in the days of the Russo-Polish War is almost identical with Marshal Pilsudski's, for Trotsky writes in 1937:

"Undoubtedly Tuchachevsky displayed extra-ordinary talents. He lacked, however, the ability to judge a military situation from every point of view. There was always an element of adventure in his strategy. For this reason we had several differences of opinion, which always, however, remained quite friendly ones. I was also compelled to criticize his attempts to create a new 'doctrine of war' by means of hastily adapted elementary Marxist formulas. We must not forget, however, that he was still very young in those days, and had made an over-rapid leap from the ranks of the Guards officers to the Bolshevist camp.

"Afterwards he may not have studied Marxism with great diligence (nobody does so nowadays in the Soviet Union), but he certainly took great pains with the art of war. He mastered the new technique, and was not unsuccessful in his rôle of mechanizer of the army. Only another war in which he was cast in advance for the rôle of generalissimo would have shown whether he had acquired the inner balance of power without which no one can become a great general."

There is but little to add to the verdicts of Pilsudski

and Trotsky. Both of them knew Tuchachevsky only in his impetuous youth. Indeed, Trotsky makes this reservation.

Tuchachevsky learnt much in the last ten years. He even made a profound study of Marxism and its revolutionary principles which Stalinism has betrayed. In the Soviet Union these works are indeed still available in unabridged, unaltered editions to persons who have climbed to as high a rung of the political ladder as Tuchachevsky did; moreover, such collections contain all the other books and treatises published abroad, including those of Trotsky.

The young Tuchachevsky spoke his mind freely. The mature man learnt to realize the value of silence. Like everyone else in the Soviet Union who has remained true to the principles of international socialism, he kept his political opinions locked away in his heart, and confided only in a few comrades of the old Bolshevist Party and the Civil War who cherished similar views. In the words of the old proverb of Tsarist days, which has once more become a living reality, he 'kept water in his mouth.'[1]

He spoke on military problems only to military audiences or to the principal political bodies of State

---

[1] This Russian proverb needs some explanation to English readers. No one can speak with water in his mouth; Russians therefore 'kept water in their mouths' in order to avoid the disaster of an over-hasty word which in Tsarist days would have led to the dungeons of the Ochrana, as it does now to those of the G.P.U. There is also a joke about the great drought in Russia, 'because 165,000,000 people keep water in their mouths.'

THE YEARS OF PEACE

and Party functionaries, to whom he had to submit his proposals and make reports on the condition of the fighting forces and the tasks of home defence. In social intercourse, however, the vitality and joy of life inherent in this Red general made him a lively exponent of the thoughts engendered by his sparkling intellect. He was also well versed in all branches of art and literature, to which he devoted such of his 'leisure hours' as were not given up to the study of history.

Herriot, the French statesman, has recorded an incident of his meeting with Tuchachevsky when on a visit to Moscow. The communicative Budyonny—that old practical warrior of the Civil War who remains a child of nature despite the height to which he has climbed in the course of his career—complained of the difficulty he experienced in the War Academy when he tried to hammer the 'great theory' into his peasant Don Cossack skull. As witness of his troubles he cited a certain 'Misha,' who happened to be standing near him. This was, in fact, Michael Tuchachevsky, who came forward and confirmed the cavalry general's statements with a smile.

Herriot tossed a military question into the conversation. Tuchachevsky answered it politely but briefly, and Herriot then found himself drawn into a discussion on Malraux's last book and the latest productions of French literature before he quite realized what had happened. The French Foreign Minister of those days thought he was indulging in flattery when he wrote that

Tuchachevsky's hair, forehead and eyes resembled those of Napoleon.

Tuchachevsky's most prominent political trait was the internationalism he expressed in his actions. For him this form of internationalism was no mere dogma or thesis, but a definite fixed opinion. The principal maxims on which his military-political opinions and actions were based never changed from those which he expressed in truly classic form in 1921:

"Outside the frontiers of the Soviet Union our Red Army should be regarded as a formation of international cadres. Every mission undertaken by our republic should be closely linked with the mission of World Revolution. That applies most particularly to our Red Army, which constitutes the first nucleus of the International Red Army. This army must be a model one in every respect, and therefore perfect in a political sense. This army must learn to forget that one national element preponderates in it; it must realize that it is the army of the international world proletariat, and nothing more. Wherever it goes, the people must be made to feel that it is a Red Army and not a Russian one."

In his mind's eyes the youthful Tuchachevsky saw this Red Army as a *fait accompli*, and so he overleapt in his plans many stages of its development. In 1921 he took steps towards the formation of an International General Staff, regarding which Trotsky wrote as follows in his treatise on *Military Doctrine*:

"Comrade Tuchachevsky applied to the Comintern

for permission to form an International General Staff within this body. Naturally this proposal came to nothing, because the time was not ripe and it was not in accordance with the mission which the 3rd World Congress had taken upon itself. Even if the Comintern had become a living force, even if strong communist organizations had come into existence in all the principal countries, such an International General Staff could only have been formed on a basis of National General Staffs, in several proletarian states. But as long as such proletarian states do not exist, an International General Staff can only be a caricature.

"Tuchachevsky thought fit to accentuate his error by printing his letter to the Comintern at the end of his interesting book *Class Warfare*. This error resembles the one he made in his violent attack on the militia army. But 'uninsured offensives' constitute one of the weak points of Comrade Tuchachevsky, who is one of our best military experts of the younger generation."

As we have already noted, Tuchachevsky was not so far wrong over this militia question. His error in the matter of the International General Staff certainly 'resembles' that which Trotsky is making to-day in attempting to create a Fourth International when international socialism can boast no parties strong enough in ideology and numbers in the principal countries of the world.

M. N. Tuchachevsky's work is as indissolubly linked with the technical efficiency achieved by the modern mechanized and motorized Red Army as Trotsky's work and personality are with the Red Army of the Civil War. But his political basic conception of the Red Army as "a buttress for the Socialist Revolution in Europe" (on the principle established by Lenin on January 12, 1918), brought him and the other internationally minded members of the Higher Command into conflict with the authorities of the Stalin régime.

Chapter Seven

The Political Aspect of the Soviet Union To-day.

Since the first Five Year Plan was begun in 1928, the social and political structure of the Soviet Union has undergone radical changes.

In that year the Soviet Union was essentially a socialist state, even though petty bourgeois methods of production predominated. Despite manifestations of bureaucratic degeneration, the dictatorship of the proletariat found in Soviet democracy a suitable means to serve as a bond between the peasants and the working classes under the leadership of the industrial proletariat. The surplus state products were distributed among working Soviet citizens on a system that approximated mainly to the socialist principle of 'To each according to his needs.' The monopoly of education formerly enjoyed by bourgeois society was abolished, while the education monopoly of a new privileged class had not yet come into existence, so that the general social order had a tendency to approximate to the second basic principle of socialism: 'From each according to his means.' The maximum salary limitation imposed on Party members (circumvented only by a small group

of Party officials who contrived to draw a second salary)
prevented the leading men of the Party and government
from losing social, cultural and economic touch with
the masses.

The deliberate trend of the Soviet Union's foreign
policy was internationalist, even though a series of
disastrous blunders and its aimless zigzag course tended
to weaken and disorganize rather than strengthen the
revolutionary movement. The internationalist nature
of this foreign policy was also manifested in the fact
that the Communist Party of the Soviet Union and the
Comintern worked in their own way (or rather, in their
own blundering way) for the revolutionizing of the
German workers and the overthrow of the German
ruling classes, even though the diplomatic relations
between the two countries were as friendly as possible
and the *leitmotif* of the Soviet Union's foreign policy
was still 'war against the Versailles system.'

1928 saw the beginnings of over-hasty industrial
developments, together with an official deathblow to
the private enterprise in trade and industry which
formed an important connecting link between the towns
and the dwellers on the plains. The peasants then began
to murmur, because these measures struck hardest at
the light industries which supplied them with articles of
everyday use.

They objected to exchanging their agricultural produce for paper roubles which could purchase neither
tools, clothing, nor industrial goods, and their protest

took the form of an attempt by the villages to starve the towns out. The Central Committee, which took its orders from Stalin, replied by decreeing the immediate collectivization of 40 per cent of all farms.

Stalin imagined that the centralized control of 40 per cent of all agricultural production would give the proletarian state sufficient foodstuffs to feed the towns and the army, and so enable it to impose its will on the remaining 60 per cent represented by 10,000,000 scattered one-family farms. But naturally the effect was just the reverse, for this collectivization was fettered by rigid dates and percentage standards and carried out without any ideological or technical preparation. It was, in fact, carried out "by means of the knout and extinguished lights," as Trotsky expressed it. The consequence was that the peasants slaughtered a large part of their livestock rather than hand it over to the *Kolkhozi*, while a considerable number of animals perished miserably on the collective farms, which then lacked the means for agricultural operations on a large scale. In order to circumvent the state's compulsory levies on produce, the peasants began to sow only as much as they required for their own personal needs.

The results of this policy were not long in making themselves manifest. The scourge of famine smote in the year 1931; in 1932 it reached its climax, and the masses of the Soviet Union found no relief until the spring of 1933.

The greatest suffering was felt in the areas where

peasants who for centuries had farmed their own land
in their own traditional ways waged the bitterest war
on the State's compulsory measures. These were the
Ukraine, the 'black earth' area of Central Russia,
Siberia and the 'bread-rich' steppes of the northern
Caucasus.

From the very beginning the fight in the Ukraine was
imbued with strong nationalist tendencies, associated
with a trend towards an autonomy movement that
aimed at an independent Soviet Ukraine within the
general state framework of the U.S.S.R. One of the
principal supporters of these efforts was Skripnik, the
old Ukrainian Communist and People's Commissar for
Education, and member of the Politburo of the Ukrainian Bolshevist Party. In 1933 he shot himself in order
to avoid arrest.

The effect on the Red Army was disastrous. In every
unit there was a mass desertion of peasant soldiers, who
hastened to their native villages, with or without their
rifles, in order to wreak vengeance on the executives of
the collective farm organizations. The peasants wrote
to their sons serving with the colours, ordering them to
go to 'Stalin, the chief of the townfolk' and demand
the restoration of their rights. Some even appealed to
their sons to return to their villages with their rifles and
help them. The Red Army was, in fact, fettered by
famine and crisis in those very months of that most
critical international situation when the German masses
had to decide between fascism and socialism, and the

state of affairs in Russia contributed in no small measure to their decision in favour of fascism. This was also the time when in the Far East political and military conditions were ripe for a successful occupation of Manchuria by the forces of Japanese imperialism.

The worst of the crisis was over in 1933. The capital invested in the heavy industries began to show its first practical results, while the light industries turned out an ever-increasing number of articles needed by the masses. Agricultural production was also on the up-grade.

But the social and political aspect of the Soviet Union had undergone a radical change in the years of crisis. In order to maintain their authority over the masses, who were called upon to endure unlimited sacrifices and privations, the heads of the State and Party machinery were forced to abolish all the outward forms of Soviet democracy. The Soviets were relieved of all their political functions, while the trade unions were practically liquidated by their amalgamation with the People's Labour Commissariat. The Party itself became an unpolitical militarized body.

In the lean years of the Civil War the important regulative task of 'distributing the privations between the classes and between workers and peasants' fell to the lot of the Bolshevist Party as the vanguard of the revolutionary proletariat. But in the lean years of 1931–3 the privations of the whole mass of the Russian people were so enormous that the machinery of the

state was forced to buy the services of a small privileged class, which could then be relied upon to carry
out its policy. The first step in this direction included
the abolition of the limitation of salaries for Party
members and the creation of a very high standard of
living for leading men of the Party and State, and the
cream of the technical intelligentsia.

When the crisis was over, the gulf between the high
standard of living of this ruling class and the low one of
the masses was widened rather than narrowed. At one
end of the social scale there was an ever-increasing
standard of comfort, while at the other, where the great
mass of the people were to be found, the standard of life
remained as low as ever.

This contrast between two standards of living has
created a new monopoly in education. Stalin adopted
the old hypocritical principle of liberal capitalism, 'From
each according to his means, to each according to his
achievements,' as a maxim of socialism, with the
proviso that the 'achievements' of a Red factory director
or Party or State official were to be appraised a hundred
and fifty times as high as those of a miner, let alone
those of a washerwoman.

This new home policy was reflected in the conduct
of foreign affairs. The foreign policy pursued by Stalin
and Litvinov took no further account of the European
and American proletariat whom Lenin termed, "the
sole, sure, reliable allies of Soviet Russia." The Soviet
Union made no more efforts to exploit the quarrels

between imperialist powers in the interests of an international socialist revolution; on the contrary, it found a home in one of the imperialist blocs, bringing as a bridal gift to this union the suspension of class warfare by the communist parties of the countries in question and propaganda by those parties in favour of the defence of their imperialist fatherlands.

These are the social and political substructures of the stage on which is enacted that 'war in the dark' which has led to the execution of Old Bolshevists and Red generals, Russia's loss of the power to act as a bulwark of international socialism, and the loss of her army's head and life.

The Execution of the Red Generals.

Throughout Soviet society and all its organizations runs the ideological cleavage between the supporters of Soviet democracy and those of the autocratic line, between the internationalists who seek their allies in the workers of the world and the oppressed colonial races and the Soviet Union patriots who desire to yoke the U.S.S.R. to the wagon of a group of imperialist powers. This cleavage does not spare the Red Army.

Tuchachevsky shared the leadership of the Soviet-democratic, internationalist line with Gamarnik, who had occupied the position of chief of the Army and Navy Political Administration since 1927. Trotsky completely misunderstands the twofold character of the

Stalinist Soviet Union, which no oligarchy can ever succeed in cutting off from its socialist basis (this could be brought about only as the result of an imperialist war, in which the Soviet Union was in alliance with a group of imperialist powers), and misunderstands equally the executed chiefs of the Red Army, of whom he writes:

"For ten years Gamarnik occupied posts of responsibility in the heart of the Party machinery; he worked in daily co-operation with the G.P.U. Under such circumstances, is it conceivable that a man should carry on two different policies—one for the outside world and one for himself? As a member of the Central Committee and the chief representative of the ruling party in the army, Gamarnik was equally with Tuchachevsky flesh of the flesh and blood of the blood of the ruling caste."

Gamarnik suffered the same fate as many old Bolshevists, such as Rykov, Bukharin and Tomsky, who were the three chief representatives of the right wing of the Communist opposition. He took a leading part in Stalin's campaign against Trotskyism, because Trotsky and his new opposition party did in fact make blunders in their attitude to a number of problems, and because he believed that Stalin's line would lead to the success of socialism. But when he reached a contrary view in 1931–3, the years of the severe crisis, and even more so in the years that followed, he began to do the only thing conceivable under the circumstances of the time in the Soviet Union—namely, to 'carry on two different policies.' One of these was certainly for the benefit of the outside world, but the other was not 'for himself,' but for a socialist liberation from the Stalin régime.

From the military point of view Tuchachevsky welcomed the industrialization and collectivization policies. A modern revolutionary army is inconceivable without a strong industrial basis, while the collective farm system enormously increased the army's fighting power because it released far more men for service at the front without injuring agricultural work and the people's food supplies than a system based on 25,000,000 peasant proprietors, each farming his own land, could ever do. Moreover, the peasant working on a collective farm learns to handle tractors and agricultural machinery, and can thus be fashioned into a good soldier more easily than the man who turns up the soil with a primitive plough.

In the years of crisis Tuchachevsky considered the bureaucratization of the land, the suppression of party democracy and the abolition of self-government in all bodies from the village community upward to the republics comprising the Soviet Union as temporary measures framed for an emergency. But when the crisis was over, this autocratic form of government was strengthened rather than diminished, and consequently the masses began to manifest silent opposition to the machinery of officialdom which they identified with the Soviet power.

This development had disastrous effects in the larger republics of the Soviet Union, such as the Ukraine, White Russia, Georgia, Armenia and Turkmenistan. There the autocratic line, enforced mainly by administrators of Great Russian origin, led to an intensification of racial antagonism engendered by the national arrogance of these officials and so strengthened the nationalistic sentiments of the inhabitants. The consequent effect on the fighting power of the Red Army in any future war would be very serious, and Gamarnik, Tuchachevsky, and other officers in responsible positions were continually haunted by the bugbear of the Austro-Hungarian Army, with its medley of nationalities, which could not stand its baptism of fire.

The demand for the reintroduction of democratic methods found yet another champion in the person of the commander of the Far Eastern Army, the present Marshal Blücher. In 1933 he succeeded in introducing important measures of democratization in the area under his control by means of a declaration (presented practically in the form of an ultimatum) that otherwise he could take no responsibility for the defence of the frontier. Thereupon the Soviet Government issued a decree which abolished the compulsory levies on all agricultural produce in that area and restored the main features of the New Economic Policy (N.E.P.).

In all matters of home policy Tuchachevsky, Gamarnik, and their friends supported the demand for a democratization of the country, which alone could create the conditions necessary for complete exploitation of the man-power in Soviet territories for purposes of national defence. With regard to foreign affairs, Russia's renunciation of her position as champion of the independence movement among the colonial races and the socialist struggle for emancipation seemed to them to threaten isolation to the Soviet Union.

Until May 1937, the active forces of the Red Army remained immune from persecution by Stalin's G.P.U., which was then commanded by Marshal Yagoda. Nevertheless, the antagonism between the Red Army and the G.P.U. was of long standing and grew continually sharper.

As chief of the latter body, Yagoda had control of a special army of 250,000 picked men. G.P.U. representatives sat on all recruiting commissions, while the physically and mentally best specimens of manhood were allotted to their forces. Their officers and men received higher pay and better rations and equipment than their comrades of the Red Army. Whenever G.P.U. formations took part in manœuvres, preliminary negotiations were invariably necessary before any sort of working agreement could be reached between the officers in command of the two bodies.

For almost ten years the Higher Command of the Red Army had carried on a campaign against this intolerable dualism in the home defence forces. Then, all of a sudden, Stalin apparently acceded to their demand, though it was not long since he had promoted

the G.P.U. chief to the rank of marshal. Meanwhile
Yagoda had won great popularity throughout the
country by his preparation of the 'cases' which led to
the execution of the old Bolshevists.

But the motives which prompted Stalin to order the
arrest of Yagoda and the liquidation of the G.P.U. as
a state within a state, were by no means in accord with
the views held by Gamarnik and Tuchachevsky. The
latter wanted to make an end of the dualistic military
system in order to suppress Yagoda's high-handed terroristic régime in the interests of Soviet democracy; Stalin,
on the other hand, eliminated the dualism of the regular
machinery of state and the G.P.U. machinery in the
interests of his own totalitarian terroristic despotism.

Stalin made use of the support he derived from the
Red Army to destroy the G.P.U. as a state within a
state; he then turned round and crushed the Soviet-
democratic internationalist opposition within the Red
Army. When examined in the course of the Piatakov
trial, Radek purchased his own life by betraying the fact
that Tuchachevsky, Gamarnik and their associates
belonged to the communist opposition. Moreover,
Stalin and Voroshilov had a score to settle with Tuchachevsky which dated from the days of the Civil War
and the Polish campaign.

Gamarnik committed suicide when about to be
arrested. Previously he had advocated the playing of a
waiting game; he also advised Piatakov to admit everything required of him by Stalin and Yagoda during his

'trial,' because he thought the leaders of the Soviet opposition ought to do everything possible to preserve their lives, since the time factor was working irresistibly for an expansion of the strength of Soviet democracy. During Piatakov's trial Gamarnik made several vain efforts to obtain clemency for him from Stalin, on the plea that the Red Army could not dispense with his co-operation in the People's Commissariat for Heavy Industries.

Tuchachevsky and the other Red generals were shot by order of Stalin. They had no 'trial,' or rather, not even the kind of proceedings that Russian custom allows to pass for a trial in such cases.

In all great political trials the Politburo decides the penalty for the accused in advance. If subsequent proceedings take place in public, they are merely a farce. A wire connects the court with Stalin's office; he follows the course of the proceedings by means of a loudspeaker and intervenes by direct communications to the presiding judge whenever he thinks fit.

In the so-called 'secret trials' the Politburo nominates the panel of judges. Their sole function, however, is to sign the protocol drawn up for them in advance.

Stalin misused the names of Budyonny and Blücher, the popular heroes of the Civil War, by appointing them to serve on the 'military court' that tried the Red Generals. He did this in order to associate them with this 'trial' in the eyes of the army and Soviet public opinion.

The accusations brought by the Stalinist oligarchy against the Red Generals are as monstrous as they are contradictory. The accused were alleged to have acted as spies on behalf of the German General Staff, to whom they offered the Ukraine and White Russia as the price of the support Germany could give them by suitable intervention in Russian home politics. They were also said to be planning the restoration of capitalism in Russia and the reinstatement of the landed proprietors in all their old powers. Finally, they were accused of planning a revolutionary war against the imperialist western powers in order to bring about a Socialist World Revolution by force of arms.

One portion of these accusations was intended for home consumption, i.e., for the citizens of the Soviet Union and the international working class. The other was for the foreign market, i.e., for the imperialist powers friendly to Russia.

Reasons of home politics required the Red Generals to be slandered as spies and advocates of the restoration of capitalism, for it was impossible to send them to execution as champions of Soviet democracy and internationalism. For the benefit of the Soviet Union's imperialist allies the bureaucracy then trumped up the charge of Tuchachevsky's 'friendly relations with Germany,' and his plan to hand over the Ukraine and White Russia (the Soviet Union's most important agricultural areas) to German Fascism.

The assertion that Tuchachevsky intended to bring

about a revolutionary war against capitalist Europe was a sop to the bourgeoisie of all nations, including both the German Fascists and the French democrats. Therewith Stalin hoped to curry general favour by posing as the representative of peace and order in Europe. His contempt of mankind is so great that he is not at all bothered by the fact that these various accusations contradict one another.

From the point of view of the ruling class which he represents, Stalin is in a position in which he could not have acted otherwise. The main function of the Soviet Union's existing machinery of state is to protect the united interest of this class (which consists of the entire State bureaucracy and the leading engineers, directors of industry, managers of collective farms, manufacturers of public opinion, etc.), against the class interests of the proletariat and against the interests of Soviet society in general, and thereby to defend the Socialist World Revolution. But since the vital interests of the Stalinist oligarchy are indissolubly linked with those of the October Revolution, i.e., with the interests of the Socialist Revolution which began in 1917 and can find its complement and completion only in the victory of the International Socialist Revolution, the Soviet Union is forced—even under Stalin's leadership—to work against the world's bourgeoisie in an objective revolutionary sense. The Soviet Union is conservative in regard to the privileges of this ruling class and counterrevolutionary in the way in which it sacrifices the interests of the working classes, but it remains a revolutionary factor in its attitude towards the bourgeoisie of the world. This essential contradiction forces the oligarchy into the unprincipled zigzag course it takes in all its political actions and utterances; it is also the starting-point for the proceedings taken against the Red Generals and for the official explanation of their 'crime.'

The Red Army was smitten to the heart by the 'trial' of its chiefs. But the 'trial' was not a cause, but merely an expression, of the severe crisis within the army, which it sharpened and intensified. As Trotsky has rightly said, the May executions in Moscow and the subsequent mass arrests and condemnations of officers of all ranks have beheaded the Red Army. Confidence in the army's fighting power has been badly shaken by the defamation and physical removal of its heads. If a Tuchachevsky, a Gamarnik, a Yakir, an Eydemann, an Uborevitch or a Primakov can be bought by Fascism, then why not also a Voroshilov, a Yegorov, a Budyonny, a Blücher or a non-political Tsarist officer such as Shaposhnikov? Why not even a Stalin? If 60 per cent of the men occupying posts at the head of the Party, the State and the Army under Lenin are spies and traitors, why not also the other 40 per cent? This is the question which every Soviet civilian and every officer and man in the Red Army must ask himself to-day. But since the army's officer corps contains few men who really believe Tuchachevsky and the other Red Generals guilty of treason, the only result of the 'trial' has been to create an unbridgeable gulf between the army and the Stalinist ruling clique.

Who are the men who will replace the executed generals? What guarantees can they give of their ability to lead the army to victory in any future war?

The most popular of the present marshals is undoubtedly Budyonny. His cavalry army was an ingenious combination of Jenghiz Khan's tactics with the elements of modern warfare. His conglomerated groups of horsemen fought with rifles and machine-guns that were carried in the old primitive waggons of the steppes. Their offensive power lay in the onslaughts they made with couched lanches and brandished sabres. Mounted on the small breed of steppe horses or on bloodstock from the Ukraine studs, they hurtled through the enemy's lines at breakneck speed as they charged over the vast steppes, whose grass "will whisper the story of how on many a starlit night and cloudy day, Budyonny's horsemen charged bravely in the fray," as the song has it.

But Budyonny has not yet shown the ability to adapt his undoubted skill to the methods of modern technique. The essential reason of his success in the Civil War may be found in the fact that he fought unentrenched opponents in the open. When Stalin and Voroshilov ordered him to attack the Lwow fortifications in 1920, his forces were decimated.

Shaposhnikov is the present Chief of the General Staff. He received a thorough military training in the

Tsarist school of war, but possesses no strategical gifts. During the Civil War he was employed as an executive for staffs at the bases, in which capacity he won distinction by his diligence and reliability, but never developed the slightest sense of initiative. In 1936 he was the head of the Russian delegation which attended the Czechoslovak manœuvres, and when proposing the health of the former Russian White Guard General Voiczechovsky, who now holds a command in the Czechoslovak army, he expressed the point of view of the typical non-political officer in the following words:

"It was just a matter of chance whether we fought for the Whites or the Reds in the Civil War."

Yegorov is a typical uneducated Tsarist officer. He speaks no language but his own. In the Civil War he won as much prominence by his military narrow-mindedness as by his personal courage. Even if he cannot be held responsible for the defeat in 1920, when he was in command of the south-western front and refused to place his forces at Tuchachevsky's disposal there is no doubt that his action was the cause of the disastrous proportions it assumed. He was appointed in May 1937, to the post formerly held by Tuchachevsky.

After Budyonny Marshal Blücher is the most popular Red Army leader. He showed military ability when commanding a division in the Civil War; in 1924 the Revolutionary Council of War sent him to China, where he worked under Borodin and became military adviser to Chiang Kai-Shek under the assumed name of

'General Galen.' Blücher-Galen reorganized the Chinese southern forces and led them victoriously to Shanghai, which city he captured when the local workers co-operated with him by organizing a revolt in the rear of the northern armies. When Marshal Chiang Kai-Shek turned traitor and massacred the Shanghai workers, he sent Borodin back to Russia, but offered General Galen wealth and honour if he would consent to remain as his adviser. When Blücher refused this offer, he was escorted to the Russian frontier with full military honours. Two years later he was in charge of the Soviet's military operations on the Manchurian frontier during the conflict in the Far East.

In 1926-7 Blücher showed great skill in the way he utilized the military backwardness of the southern Chinese armies to defeat the equally backward troops of the northern forces. In 1929 he defeated the Chinese troops by a series of swift and vigorous operations. But this latter campaign gives no standard by which to test the Red Army's fighting strength or Blücher's ability in a war against modernized forces.

In 1929 the Chinese soldiers fought very unwillingly against the Russian troops. In August 1937, the same Chinese forces displayed extraordinary heroism when inspired by their profound and justifiable hatred against the armies of Japanese imperialism. But the technical and tactical superiority of the Japanese army over the Chinese is no less than the Russian technical and tactical superiority of 1929.

Russian home defence has been undermined by the 'trial' and subsequent disorganization of the Red Army. The bureaucracy should have been aware of this risk when they ordered the execution of the Red Generals. Did they then feel themselves so strong that they could afford to disregard the upheaval it was bound to cause all over the country?

The internal stability of an autocratic régime can seldom be gauged before its overthrow. Robespierre sent one opposition leader after another to the guillotine. There seemed to be no limits to his power; he had Danton, the great tribune of the people, beheaded, and no hand was raised to save his victim. Then, suddenly, on a trivial issue dealing with the question of the arrest of some insignificant person, the machinery of State broke down in Robespierre's hands. The Convention arrested him, and when his head fell under the guillotine's blade, the only man to stand up for the revolutionary dictator and die with him was Saint-Just. But this comparison between Robespierre's France and Stalin's Russia is applicable only to the valuation of the stability of two autocratic dictatorships.

It is not a consciousness of strength, but rather a feeling of insecurity, that impels the Stalinist oligarchy to exterminate all those persons who might serve as focal points for the struggle of the socialist masses for power in the event of a crisis.

After the October Revolution many Russian monarchists reproached themselves bitterly for having failed

to strike off all the heads of the 'hydra of revolution'
at the right time, for there had been a period when they
had all the revolutionary leaders, without exception, in
the power of the Tsarist Ochrana. But the Stalinist
bureaucrats have learnt a lesson from the belated
wisdom of these monarchists.

As far back as 1921 the Kronstadt Mutiny disclosed
the fact that the masses of the people (who showed their
sympathy with the mutineers by their strikes) only
refrained from overthrowing the Bolshevist Government because there was no other organized socialist
body in the country. The crisis of 1931–3 revealed the
full magnitude of the danger to the Stalinist clique. It
was only averted because the old opposition leaders
Zinoviev, Kamenev, Piatakov, Tomsky, Rykov, Bukharin and Sokolnikov agreed to sink their differences
with the Stalinist régime for the time being in view of
the deadly perils of crisis, famine, and imminent war
that beset the land.

The masses in a totalitarian state are deprived of even
the smallest vestiges of political power, and so a
moment of crisis finds them unable to produce from
their ranks any organizations ready and able to do
battle on their behalf. They can only apply for assistance to groups already formed and persons possessing
some sort of authority.

By means of the 'proceedings' taken against the
leaders of the Bolshevist Old Guard and the Red Army,
the present government intends to insure its totali-

tarianism against any new crisis into which a future war would throw the country. That is why it shoots not merely the visible representatives of Soviet-democratic and internationalist tendencies, but also those thousands of unknown communist workers, Party organizers, industrialists and officers, in fact all the little Tuchachevskys and Piatakovs whom it accuses of espionage for Germany or Japan or 'Trotskyist sabotage.'

The execution of Tuchachevsky and the other Red Generals was a definite war measure undertaken by the Stalinist bureaucracy, whose aim was to exterminate along with the many possible rallying-points for a struggle for power in the event of a future war. But in consolidating the state of affairs that gives them power, they are undermining the foundations of socialist society and so destroying the very conditions of their own existence.

Perspectives and Future Tasks.

Such, then, is the position twenty years after the October Revolution. Despite the huge expansion of its technical basis and despite the mechanization of the Red Army, the Soviet Union's stability has been imperilled by Stalin's policy more than it ever was in the days of the Civil War. Lenin's internationalist policy rendered the imperialist powers incapable of warlike action against the Soviet Union, but Stalin's narrow nationalist policy and the disorganization occasioned within the ranks of the international working class movement by the Comintern's policy, have made it impossible for the proletariat of the imperialist countries to prevent any criminal war against the Soviet Union. The danger threatening the working classes by reason of Stalin's present policy is all the greater by virtue of the fact that he carries it out in the name of Lenin. But he is only using an old, well-proven recipe, for in 1915 Lenin wrote in his polemic against the leaders of the Second International and their policy of centralism:

"History shows us that after the death of any revolutionary leader who has won popularity with the masses his enemies appropriate his name and use it to hoodwink the oppressed classes."

The only conditions under which a country's manpower and entire economic potentialities can be completely exploited for war purposes, are those which imply a democratization of the country and the elimination of all conflicts between the masses and their rulers and between the various nationalities that make up the state. But an autocratic government accentuates these conflicts, disorganizes the economic system, and deprives the masses of all power of initiative. In any future war the victory will go to the belligerent with 'the better nerves,' provided, of course, that he has a sufficiency of material and mental resources. But an autocrat brings elements of unrest and nervousness into the machinery of the army, industry and state by virtue of his personal intervention in all their affairs.

An instance of this may be seen in the way Stalin ignored the protests of the aircraft constructors when he ordered them to build the huge aeroplane known as the 'Maxim Gorky' in 'record time and with a luxury hitherto unknown.' This machine was to fly over Moscow on February 23, 1934, the Anniversary of the Red Army, but when the pilot tried to take off from the October Field on the appointed day, he was unable to get it off the ground. The whole construction of the machine had to be overhauled for two months.

On May 1 the Maxim Gorky made its appearance in the sky, amid the plaudits of the populace. The machine was designed to provide a flying headquarters for the general staff in the event of a war on two fronts that might be 10,000 kilometres apart and so to keep the higher command in close contact with both groups of armies, but the inexperience of its designers in the construction of huge machines of this type and the various alterations that had to be undertaken in order to get it into the air on the appointed day had made it such a fragile bird that Tuchachevsky refused to take it over for the army. When the disaster which the experts foresaw was brought about by a slight collision with another machine that touched one of its wing-tips —a hit by an anti-aircraft battery would have produced the same effect—Stalin promptly thwarted the plans of the aircraft industry by ordering twelve giant machines of the same type.

One of the most important requisites for a successful

mobilization is a well-organized system of rail transport; this is even more necessary in the Soviet Union than in other countries, because the railway network is a bad one, with extremely wide meshes. But even in peace-time the Soviet railways are very badly run.

Kaganovitch tried to raise their standard by a system of rewards, as well as by executions for 'sabotage.' But he did not go to the root of the trouble, for the per-manent way is in a miserable condition. Most of it has been left in the same state as it was when taken over from Tsarism, to which must be added the deterioration caused by twenty years of wear and tear. The wage standards of the railwaymen are extremely low, save for a few privileged persons in receipt of Stakhanov wages. In 1935 Kolzov published the results of a medical enquiry into the condition of thirty engine-drivers accused of negligence which had caused collisions; all were found to be undernourished, while 80 per cent were tubercular subjects. All told the court that they were in a state of complete physical exhaustion when the accidents occurred.

Such is the state of the railways in time of peace. But in 1934 the Soviet Government ordered a trial mobili-zation of the Siberian railways. The result was disas-trous, for in two days the entire traffic was in a state of such helpless chaos that gigantic efforts were needed to restore the ordinary peace time-table. In this regard we may add that the trouble was by no means due to the nature of the mobilization scheme, which was perfectly capable of realization.

Lenin was fond of poking fun at the 'Asiatic sloven-liness' of the Russians by the following anecdote. In the early days of the World War, when America was still neutral, a Yankee visited the belligerent countries. In Halle he enquired when the next express train left for Berlin, and was told: "At 12 minutes and 26 seconds past 2 p.m." Then, on expressing his amazement at such accuracy, he was told by the stationmaster: "But, my dear sir, there's a war on." Afterwards he went to Russia and wanted to catch a train from Saratov to Moscow. But the stationmaster at Saratov merely scratched his head. "The Moscow express, eh?" he said. "Well, it ought to have been here long ago. It's 4 p.m. now, and if the train gets in before 8, and if we can manage to find an engine for it, it may leave to-night." The American was horrified. "But, my dear sir, there's a war on," the stationmaster reminded him.

To-day the phlegmatic 'Asiatic slovenliness' is still far from vanquished. But at present it is in abeyance, and in its place we have the nervousness, indecision and fear that an autocratic government brings with it.

Even now, in peace-time, the conjunction of a thirst for record figures and a panicky dread of responsibility has brought the economic life of the whole country into a feverish condition. To-day industrial concerns work to 100 per cent capacity, but the output of many important industries is still a long way under normal.

This is partly due to objective reasons. The plans are

too ambitious. But one essential cause of their non-fulfilment is to be found in the psychological effects of this autocratic, terroristic régime. The methods of intimidation it employs will produce no pioneers of industry, but only petty, scared, indecisive officials with no sense of initiative.

These criticisms of the whole machinery of State and industry may be applied with even greater force to the army. "A modern army," wrote Lenin in 1915, in his essay, *The Collapse of the Second International*, "is a model organization. This organization is good only when it combines elasticity with the art of endowing millions of men with a single will. When a million men inspired by one single will for some particular purpose, can change the nature of their groupings and actions, the localities and methods of those actions, and their weapons and tools—all in accordance with the changing conditions and needs of warfare—then we have something that can be defined as organization."

Modern warfare, which may leave a man entirely to his own resources on the battlefield and demand from the private a power of decision equal to that required of a general in the wars of past centuries, presupposes a high sense of initiative and great willingness to take responsibility that can only be evolved in a truly democratic society, i.e. in a socialistic state in which all class differences and racial antagonisms have been abolished. A modern army and an autocratic régime mix as well as fire and water.

In 1928 I told Blücher that his best ally in the Chinese campaign was the German Colonel Bauer, who when serving as instructor to the Chinese northern forces made his soldiers practise the goose-step. This step presupposes the type of military organization, the general political structure of State and army, and the form of discipline—or rather, 'kadaver' discipline—with which Frederick the Great won his victories under the tactical and technical conditions of the eighteenth century. But it bodes destruction in advance to any army of the twentieth century which has to fight the modern forces of an up-to-date opponent.

In the above-quoted polemic against the Second International, Lenin said that: "the living soul of Marxism is its revolutionary spirit." He stigmatized the 'lifeless Marxism' of the patriotic socialists and centralists. The living soul of the Red Army is its revolutionary, international spirit, but Stalin's policy killed the Red Army long before he beheaded it by executing its leaders.

The decisive factor is no longer the possession of a hundred aircraft or a thousand tanks more or less than the enemy (important though this factor undeniably is), but a diversion of policy from the autocratic to the Soviet-democratic line, from the rotting soil of narrow-minded nationalism and arrogance to the firm foundation of revolutionary internationalism. Tuchachevsky and Gamarnik, who realized this and so began to turn their minds to politics, had to pay for their insight and their devotion to the socialist cause with their lives. Their deaths were a heavy loss to the international working class, but far more is at stake—the October Revolution itself!

The Bolshevists won the Civil War because they succeeded in creating the political and social-economic preliminary conditions they needed for the seizure and maintenance of power. But the Red Army will only win a future war with some imperialist power, and the Soviet Union will only emerge from such a war as a Socialist, Soviet State, if the Russian proletariat succeeds in creating the right preliminary conditions for such a victory.

The centre of gravity of Soviet home defence has shifted from the military to the political sphere. History therefore, has once more caused the military problem to become the essence of the political problem.

Chapter Eight

The last lines of the foregoing work were written in November 1937. Since that time the events of the last four months (and most especially the Bukharin–Rykov "trial") have thrown considerable new light on the present state of the Red Army and the aims and objects of its executed leaders. I therefore owe a debt of gratitude to my English publisher, for although my book was just about to appear, he has kindly permitted me to include this addendum, which is based on the latest official Russian statements and certain private information. A portion of the latter has been supplied to me by officers belonging to the Tuchachevsky group.

I propose to deal first with the above-mentioned "trial." The accusations, which evoked the same profuse display of false pathos from the public prosecutor and the defendants, implicated the Tuchachevsky–Gamarnik group in two main directions. With regard to home politics, they were said to have aimed at plotting to overthrow the Soviet régime and restore capitalism, while their foreign policy amounted to acts of high treason committed for the benefit of British,

German, Japanese and Polish imperialism. Taking this last charge first, we find that the high treason committed by the leaders of the Red Army dates back to the year 1920, according to "evidence" obtained by the highest Soviet court. It is thus almost as old as the Soviet Republic and the Red Army.

The official protocol of the 'trial' contains the following statement by Krestinsky, who was the Soviet ambassador to Berlin for so many years:

"In 1921 Trotsky suggested to me that I should endeavour to obtain from Seeckt a regular financial subsidy to him (Trotsky) for the development of his illegal activities. Trotsky also told me that if Seeckt required him to earn the money by espionage work, I could and must agree. I therefore broached the question to Seeckt and mentioned a sum of 250,000 gold marks (i.e. 60,000 dollars) a year. Thereupon Seeckt discussed the matter with the Chief of the German General Staff and afterwards told me that he agreed in principle. He said that Trotsky's share of the bargain would be to supply him with reliable confidential information of a military nature, which he could transmit either direct from Moscow or through me in Berlin."

Trotsky did this. When Vishinsky asked Krestinsky how much money he obtained altogether in this fashion, he received the reply:

"From 1923 to 1930 we received yearly cash payments of 250,000 gold marks."

"About 2,000,000 gold marks altogether then?" Vishinsky asked, and added the further question: "But was not your Trotskyist organization in touch with Seeckt even before 1921?"

KRESTINSKY: They were in touch with one another, but I would rather not say anything about that in open court.

VISHINSKY: Can you tell me who Kopp was?

KRESTINSKY: Kopp was an old Menshevist who was very intimate with Trotsky.

VISHINKSY: But did not Kopp get in touch with Seeckt as far back as 1920 and discuss with him this very point on which you decline to say anything except in a secret session?

KRESTINSKY: Yes, Seeckt approached Kopp.

VISHINSKY: From which I deduce the fact that these negotiations began before 1921 or 1922. He sought an approach to Seeckt in 1920 and found it via Kopp.

Monstrous and incredible though it may sound, this is one of the episodes in the "trial" which has a certain "approximation" to the truth.

It is perfectly true that Seeckt approached Trotsky in July 1920, through the intermediacy of Kopp, who was then Soviet ambassador in Berlin. It is equally true that Krestinsky continued these negotiations in 1921 and that an agreement was reached in 1922, by which the German Reichswehr transmitted the leaders of the Red Army via Krestinsky yearly payments amounting to the aforesaid 250,000 gold marks. It is furthermore true that Trotsky, alias the Peoples' Commissariat for War, facilitated visits to Russia for "agents of the German Reichswehr" or—to put it more accurately—active officers of the German Reichswehr and retired officers of the old German army ("Black Reichswehr"). These German officers carried on con-

spiratorial activities on Soviet territory continually
from 1923 to 1930. These are the facts, but their
significance is precisely the opposite of that alleged in
the "trial."

What, then, is the whole truth?

When the Red Army advanced on Warsaw in July
1920 under Tuchachevsky's leadership and "the
imperialist system built upon the Treaty of Versailles
began to creak in every joint," as Lenin remarked on
October 15, 1920, Seeckt approached the Soviet
Government through Kopp and made suggestions for
co-operation between the German Reichswehr and the
Red Army "against Versailles." According to Lenin,
"that was the time when everyone in Germany, including the blackest reactionaries and monarchists, declared
that the Bolshevists would be their salvation." Lenin
also gives the following description of the mood prevailing in Germany during the Russian advance on
Warsaw:

> "A curious type of reactionary-revolutionary has
> come into existence in Germany. We find an example
> of him in the raw lad from East Prussia who said that
> Wilhelm must be brought back because there was no
> law and order in Germany, but that the Germans must
> march with the Bolshevists." (Lenin's speech on
> 22 September, 1920.)

It was only the sudden turn of the tide of war and the
collapse of the Russian offensive when within sight of
Warsaw which prevented the negotiations between
Seeckt and the Soviet Government from reaching a

definite agreement in 1920. In the following year Krestinsky resumed conversations with Seeckt at the instance of his government, i.e., Lenin and Trotsky, but the preliminary conditions required for a secret military agreement between the Red Army and the Reichswehr did not come into existence until Germany and the Soviet Union concluded the Treaty of Rapallo in 1922.

This secret agreement led to the establishment of a flying-school for German officers at Ljuberzi, a village twenty-one kilometres distant from Moscow. Furthermore, German officers of all ranks underwent courses in tank work, heavy artillery work and in the co-operation of these with other arms, since the Treaty of Versailles forbade the German Army the use of tanks, heavy artillery or military aircraft. The administrative department of the Red Army supplied the instructors and received the yearly sum of 250,000 gold marks from the heads of the Reichswehr, while the supply of aircraft and other materials was regulated by another special agreement.

When Hitler came to power, Tuchachevsky and Gamarnik demanded the immediate suspension of military relations with the German Reichswehr. Stalin did not agree with them, because he was still minded to base his foreign policy on a Berlin–Moscow axis. All the old Soviet diplomats (and more especially Krestinsky, Karachan and Sokolnikov) wanted to break off diplomatic relations with Germany after the Reichstag Fire and the subsequent accusations made by

Hitler and Goering against the Soviet Union, but despite
their protests the Peoples' Commissariat for Foreign
Affairs, which was then ruled by Litvinov, carried on the
former anti-Versailles policy for almost another two
years; meanwhile the Versailles system collapsed,
although it was not the blows of the Proletarian
Revolution and the Red Army which caused its down-
fall, but the fury of the Fascist offensive.

The secret agreement between the Reichswehr and the
Red Army was not cancelled until Hitler abolished it in
1935. By that time it had accomplished its purpose of
providing Germany with the specialists she required to
train an air force, a tank corps and heavy artillerymen.

The German flying-school at Ljuberzi was likewise
not liquidated until 1935. In the summer of 1933 an
excited Russian flying officer told me the following
characteristic episode.

Shortly after the Reichstag Fire he said to some
Reichswehr officers in Ljuberzi: "We Russians are a set
of idiots! We have trained Hitler's officers for him, and
he will show his gratitude in the form of bombs dropped
over Moscow!"

"No, not over Moscow," replied the military airmen
of the Reich. "Over Paris! Yes, over Paris!"

In the "trial" the charge of persistent high treason was
brought against Trotsky and the group led by Tuchachevsky and Gamarnik. As this was based on the
history of the Treaty of Rapallo and its secret military
agreement, I have found it necessary to deal with this

episode in detail. All the other accusations of intrigues with foreign powers which were made against the executed Red Generals (i.e., their negotiations with Trotsky and the Reichswehr between 1934 and 1937) emanate from the brains of Stalin and Yeshov, so that it is not worth while wasting words on them.[1]

Like the other genuine leaders of the Communist opposition and the sham ones whom Stalin manœuvred into power for his own purposes, the Red Generals were also accused of intrigues and conspiracies at home. Here again we find a similar basis of truth in the charges.

According to the official documents pertaining to the "trial," it would appear that "the military group led by Tuchachevsky and Gamarnik were inveigled into the conspiracy by Piatakov on Trotsky's behalf at the end of 1933." Krestinsky was alleged to have made contact with the leaders of the Red Army in 1934, but it was also stated that Tuchachevsky got in touch with Rykov, Bucharin, Tomsky and their followers as far back as 1930, when he also negotiated with Rudsutak, who had held the post of deputy-chairman of the Council of Peoples' Commissars for a number of years. The home-political programme of all these various opposition groups was said to comprise the restoration of capitalism, the reinstatement of the landed proprietors and even the partition of the Soviet Union.

The official documents cite a number of variations in

---

[1] It is not within the scope of the present work to discuss the complicated system of cross-examination which elicited statements from the accused. This will form the subject of a later work.

the plans formulated by these conspirators for the over-throw of the Soviet Government. Their initial activities tended towards the promotion of mass revolts, in which they attained some partial success in the years 1931-4, when rebellions broke out in the Ukraine, the Northern Caucasus and Western Siberia. But these isolated risings led to no decisive victory.

In 1934 they were said to have evolved a plan to arrest all the delegates to the Party Day. The execution of this plan was entrusted to "the groups led by Tuchachevsky and Yagoda," but, according to Rykov's evidence, the conspirators were daunted by "the resolute attitude of the Party, the popularity of the Government and the absence of even the slightest signs of discontent in the country." This statement sounds somewhat strange, because Rykov's position as one of the leaders of the conspiracy should have enabled him to know that two-thirds of the Government of the U.S.S.R. were in the plot, along with five-sixths of the government of White Russia and the Ukraine, and nine-tenths of the government of Turkestan, since these percentages of the members of the above Governments were arrested, and many of them were subsequently shot.

Be that as it may, the delegates to the Party Day were not arrested, and consequently the conspirators decided to exploit a war situation, i.e., in the event of hostilities they decided to "open the front" to the troops of the German and Japanese Fascists with whom they had allied themselves. But despite all the promises made to them by Trotsky, the German Reichswehr and the Japanese General Staff, the war did not materialize, whereupon they turned their thoughts towards a "palace revolution." Tuchachevsky was "to assemble a number of conspiring generals in his quarters; then they were to force their way into the Kremlin on some excuse or other, occupy its telephone exchange and murder the members of the Government and Party leaders." All this is vouched for in the confession made by Rosenholtz; moreover, we learn that "Gamarnik proposed to occupy the building of the People's Commissariat for Home Affairs (i.e., the G.P.U.) during the military *coup d'état*. It was his intention to carry out this plan with the assistance of some body of troops which he would lead in person, for he assumed that his status as an old Party leader and politician would give him sufficient authority over the men."

These, then, are the charges contained in the official documents. Let us see how far they correspond to the actual truth.

According to reliable sources of information, there was actually a plan for a "palace revolution" and the overthrow of Stalin's dictatorship by forcible means. It is also true that the Red Army was allotted a decisive role in the execution of this plan, which was to be carried out under the leadership of Tuchachevsky and Gamarnik. The Moscow Proletarian Rifle Division, led by General Petrovsky, a son of the President of the Ukrainian Soviet Republic, was to occupy the Kremlin and break the resistance of the G.P.U. troops, which were commanded by Yagoda until the autumn of 1936, when Yeshov took his place. The conspirators reckoned on the support of the workers and the benevolent neutrality of the peasants; in the event of stiffening resistance from the motorized and excellently armed G.P.U. Army, Ukrainian troops commanded by General Dubovoi were to be rushed into Moscow.

The date of this "palace revolution" was repeatedly postponed on account of the misgivings of the conspirators, who feared that the temporary internal disorder caused by the overthrow of Stalin's dictatorship might be exploited by imperialism in general and the Germans and Japanese in particular. When Piatakov and his comrades were brought to trial in January, 1937, Radek gave hints of Tuchachevsky's associations with the Communist Opposition group. Thereupon the date of the rising was finally fixed for the middle of May, but Stalin and Yeshov thus gained time to take countermeasures. Tuchachevsky, Gamarnik and several hundred officers of high rank were arrested in the early weeks of May, and some of them, including Petrovsky and Dubovoi, were promptly shot.

Then if there was really a plan for a rebellion, was not Stalin justified in putting the conspirators on trial for high treason and shooting them? From the standpoint of the maintenance of his dictatorship as well as from the standpoint of the privileged class in whose name he exercised his dictatorship, the answer must be in

the affirmative. But a true Socialist cannot appraise
political struggles for power from the standpoint of
formal legal rights. For him the only question can be:
was this rising to be carried out in the interest of the
progress of humanity, i.e., in the interest of Socialism,
or against it?

His main consideration must therefore be the aims
and objects put forward by the opposition group within
the Communist Party and their representatives in the Red
Army under Tuchachevsky's leadership; the methods
by which they proposed to accomplish those aims and
objects can only occupy a secondary place. But one
point is clear: when a totalitarian government annihi-
lates with fire and sword any manifestation of opposition
in any form, there is no possibility of carrying out a
political programme by democratic means.

Even the methods by which the trial was conducted
could not prevent the true aims of the Communist
Opposition trickling through in occasional drops.
When, for instance, Vishinsky enquired what Bukharin
imagined to be the future development of the Soviet
Union under Stalin's leadership, the author of the
Communist International's programme replied: "We
prognosticated a trend towards capitalism." When
warned by Vishinsky, he added in the tones of a school-
boy who has learnt his lesson: "We were mistaken, for it
was leading to a complete victory for Socialism."

The axis around which all political problems of the
Communist Opposition revolved was the restoration of

the Soviet democracy which they deemed the most important basis and only guarantee for a remodelling of society in a socialistic sense. By Soviet democracy they implied the rebuilding of the Party and the Trade Unions as instruments and forms of expression of a working-class democracy. "All power to the Soviets!" was their slogan. Soviet democracy must therefore imply also a return to Lenin's national policy of political self-government for the various Socialist Soviet Republics comprising the Soviet Union, while the realization of Soviet democracy would inevitably involve the abolition of the political and economic privileges given to the ruling class under Stalin's régime. As, however, the latter had no intention of relinquishing these privileges voluntarily, there remained no other ways and means to induce them to do so except by those of a forcible nature.

The programme by which the Communist Opposition planned to accomplish the restoration of Soviet democracy was roughly the following.

I. In the Sphere of Industry. To force the development of the ready-made goods industry in order to satisfy the needs of the urban and rural masses and thus stimulate agricultural production by natural means instead of administrative compulsory measures. The heavy industries which have been built up at the cost of excessive sacrifices are now able, on the whole, to meet the demands of national economy, even from the standpoint of national defence. Steel is not the only material needed for the prosecution of a war; butter, boots and clothing are also required. The Communist Opposition therefore proposed to put a brake on the investment of capital in new heavy industry undertakings and to put an immediate end to gigantic luxury buildings, such as the Moscow "Palace of the Soviets," for the erection of which a sum has been earmarked that is twice the amount devoted to the establishment of the Magneto-gorsk Combine (mining and heavy industry), which gives employment and housing to 200,000 workers.

To relax the foreign trade monopoly for products of the ready-made goods industry which cannot be manu-factured in sufficient quantities within the U.S.S.R. Such a relaxation took place in 1931–4, although it was not the masses who benefited by it but only the privi-leged owners of gold, foreign currency or special coupons, who were able to purchase foreign foodstuffs, textile goods, motor-cars, etc., in the State's Torgsin shops (shops for foreign goods). But this time the relaxation was not to benefit the privileged classes but rather serve the needs of the masses.

II. In the Sphere of Agriculture. Application of the principle of genuine liberty for the peasants to belong to collective farms or cultivate their own land as one-man farms. Peasants belonging to collective farms would be then permitted to choose what form of collectivity they preferred to adopt, i.e., any form between the comparatively mild kind known as the 'Artel,' in which only some means of production (such as tractors) are collectivized, and the agricultural community.

III. In the Sphere of Foreign Policy. "Activization of Foreign Policy" was a slogan which enjoyed great popularity in the ranks of the Red Army and among the broad masses of the Soviet youth, as is apparent from the well-known letter addressed to Stalin by "the Propagandist of the Ivanov Communist Youth Association." But the reader will ask what exactly did the Communist Opposition mean by "Activization of Foreign Policy."

When Hitler came into power a wave of intense bitterness and shame swept through the ranks of the Red Army, who were indignant at the idea that economic deterioration rendered the Soviet Union impotent to carry out "an active foreign policy" in reply to the impudent Fascist provocation it was receiving. Red officers were "in despair" at the meek spirit in which the Soviet Government swallowed all the provocations of Japanese imperialism and thus sacrificed the Chinese Revolution. The phrase "opening the front" was coined to express the passivity of the Soviet foreign policy towards Japanese aggression, i.e., Stalin was considered to have "opened the front" of the Chinese Revolution to Japanese imperialism. In the "trial" this phrase assumed quite a different significance, for it was interpreted in the sense that Tuchachevsky intended to open the front line of the Red Army to the forces of German and Japanese imperialism in the event of war.

The Spanish Civil War gave a vigorous impulse to the desire for "activization of foreign policy." At the time of its outbreak a storm of indignation swept through the whole country; although Stalin delayed action for three months, it eventually forced him to "open a valve" and assist the Spanish Government with certain supplies of arms in return for political concessions (war on Trotskyism).

The activization of the Soviet foreign policy in dealing with Japanese imperialism and German and Italian Fascism (Abyssinia and Spain) and promoting the Socialist World Revolution, was and still is the foreign political programme of the Tuchachevsky–Gamarnik group within the Red Army.

Appendix 1

THE SCHEME FOR A SOCIALIST ARMY

(Decree issued by the Council of People's Commissars on January 15, 1918)

The old army was a class instrument in the hands of the bourgeoisie for the oppression of the workers. The seizure of power by the workers and propertyless persons renders necessary the formation of a new army. The tasks of this new army will be the defence of the Soviet authority, the creation of a basis for the transformation of the standing army into a force deriving its strength from a nation in arms, and, furthermore, the creation of a basis for the support of the coming Socialist Revolution in Europe.

I

The Council of People's Commissars has decided to organize the new army as a 'Red Army of Workers and Peasants' on the following basis:

1. The Red Army of Workers and Peasants will be formed from the class-conscious and best elements of the working classes.

2. All citizens of the Russian Republic who have

completed their eighteenth year are eligible for service. Service in the Red Army is open to anyone ready to give his life and strength for the defence of the achievements of the October Revolution, the Soviet Power and Socialism. Enlistment in the Red Army is conditional upon guarantees being given by a military or civil committee functioning within the territory of the Soviet Power or by Party or Trade Union committees or, in extreme cases, by two persons belonging to one of the above organizations. Should an entire unit desire to join the Red Army, its acceptance is conditional upon a collective guarantee and the affirmative vote of all its members.

II

1. The families of members of the Red Army of Workers and Peasants will be maintained by the State and receive, in addition, a monthly supplement of 50 roubles.

2. Members of soldiers' families who are incapable of work and have hitherto been supported by the aforesaid soldiers will receive further support in accordance with the local cost of living, as determined by the local Soviets.

III.

The Council of People's Commissars is the supreme head of the Red Army of Workers and Peasants. The immediate command and administration of the Army is vested in the Commissariat for Military Affairs and in the Special All-Russian College therein contained.

The President of the Council of People's Commissars:
V. ULYANOV-LENIN.

The Commander-in-Chief:
N. KRYLENKO.

The People's Commissars for War and the Fleet:
DYBENKO, PODVOISKY.

The People's Commissars:
PROSHYAN, SAMOISKY, STEINBERG.

For the Bureau of People's Commissars:
VLADIMIR BONTSCH-BRUYEVITCH.

SCHEME FOR COMPULSORY MILITARY TRAINING

(Published in No. 83 of the "Isvestia" of the All-Russian Central Executive Committee of the Soviets, April 26, 1918)

The liberation of mankind from the burden of militarism and the barbarity of war between nations, is one of the basic tasks of socialism. The aims of socialism are universal disarmament, perpetual peace and the fraternal co-operation of all races inhabiting the world.

These aims will be accomplished when power is transferred to the hands of the workers in all powerful capitalist countries, when all means of production have been taken out of the hands of the exploiters and made over to the workers for the common good, and when a communist order of society has created a firm basis of human solidarity.

At present Russia is the only country in which the
State authority is vested in the workers. The imperialist
bourgeoisie is still in power in all other countries. Its
policy is directed towards the suppression of Communist Revolution and the enslavement of all weak
races. The Russian Soviet Republic is surrounded by
enemies on all sides and must therefore create a
powerful army, under the protection of which the
communistic transformation of the country's social
order may be accomplished.

The Republic's Government of Workers and Peasants has set itself the immediate task of enrolling all
citizens for compulsory labour and military service.
In this work it has encountered obstinate resistance
from the bourgeoisie, who refuse to renounce their
economic privileges and are trying to recapture the
reins of government by means of conspiracies, insurrec-
tions, and treasonable agreements with foreign imperialists.

To arm the bourgeoisie would be tantamount to
provoking a continuous internal war within the ranks
of the army and so crippling the army's strength for war
against external foes. The usurious, exploiting portion
of society which is unwilling to assume the same rights
and duties as the rest must not be allowed to obtain
arms. The Government of Workers and Peasants will
find means to impose on the bourgeoisie in some form
or other a part of the burden of the defence of the
Republic, which has been forced by the crimes of the

possessing classes to endure these heavy trials and necessities. But in the immediate transition period military training and the bearing of arms must be restricted to workers and peasants who employ no outside labour.

Citizens between eighteen and forty years of age who have undergone the prescribed military training will be registered as liable to military service. They are required to answer the first summons of the Government of Workers and Peasants to fill up the cadres of the Red Army, which have been formed of devoted soldiers, ready to sacrifice themselves for the freedom and independence of the Russian Soviet Republic and the International Socialist Revolution.

Male citizens of the Russian Federated Soviet Republic are liable to undergo military training :

(1) During school age, the lower limit of which will be determined by the People's Commissariat for Education.

(2) During the preparatory age, from sixteen to eighteen years.

(3) During the age of obligatory military service, from eighteen to forty years.

Female citizens will be trained only with their own consent, in accordance with the general practice.

N.B.—Persons whose religious convictions forbid the use of arms will be liable only to forms of training that exclude the use of arms.

(1) The People's Commissar for War is responsible for the training of men in the obligatory military and preparatory ages. The People's Commissar for Education, working in close co-operation with the People's Commissar for War, is responsible for the training of boys of school age.

(2) All workmen employed in factories and workshops, on farms and on the land, and all peasants who exploit no outside labour are liable to undergo training.

(3) The military commissariats (of the districts, governments, circuits and Volosts) will supervise the compulsory military training in their respective localities.

(4) Conscripts receive no compensation during their periods of training. The periods of training must be arranged in such a way as to cause the minimum interference with the conscripts' regular occupations.

(5) The period of training is for six consecutive weeks, with a minimum of twelve hours per week. The period of training for special corps and the sequence of repetitive training will be determined by special enactments.

(6) Persons who have already undergone training in the regular army may be exempted from further training on passing a suitable test. They will then be required to fill in the discharge papers generally issued to all persons who have undergone their compulsory training.

(7) Training will be given by competent instructors in accordance with the programme drawn up by the People's Commissar for War.

(8) Whosoever evades compulsory military training
or is negligent in the performance of it will be liable to
prosecution.

Regulations for War Commissars

A War Commissar is a direct political representative
of the Soviet Government with the army. His post has
a special significance. Commissars' posts will be
assigned only to irreproachable revolutionaries who
have the ability to remain incarnations of revolutionary
duty at critical moments and under the most difficult
circumstances.

The War Commissar's person is inviolate. An insult
offered to a War Commissar engaged in the performance of his duty or any act of violence committed
against a War Commissar will be deemed equivalent to
the greatest of crimes against the Soviet Power of the
Republic. It is the duty of a War Commissar to prevent
the army from showing disrespect to the Soviet
authority and to prevent army institutions from becoming nests of conspiracy or employing weapons against
workmen and peasants. A War Commissar takes part
in all the activities of the commanding officer to whom
he is attached; these two persons must receive reports
and sign orders jointly. Validity is ascribed only to
those orders of a War Soviet which bear the signature
of at least one Commissar in addition to that of the
commanding officer.

All work must be done under the eyes of the Commissar. The only work which he does not undertake is the special military leadership, which is the task of the military expert with whom he co-operates.

Commissars are not responsible for the appropriateness of orders given for purely military, operative purposes. The entire responsibility for these falls on the military commander. The Commissar's signature to an operative order implies that he guarantees the said order to be one dictated by purely operative (and not counter-revolutionary) reasons. If a Commissar cannot approve of a military order, he must not veto it, but must report his opinion of it to the War Soviet immediately superior to his own. A Commissar may prevent the execution of a military order only when he has justifiable grounds for belief that it is inspired by counter-revolutionary motives.

An order receives the force of law when it has been signed by a Commissar, and must then be executed at all costs. It is the Commissar's duty to see that all orders are carried out to the letter, for which purpose he is invested with all the authority and all the means of the Soviet Power. Commissars who connive at the non-execution of orders will be forthwith removed from their posts and prosecuted.

Commissars must maintain intact the connection between the institutions of the Red Army and the central and local organizations of the Soviet Government, and assure the support of these organizations to the Red Army.

Commissars must see that all ranks of the Red Army do their duty conscientiously and energetically, that all money expenditure is economical and under the strictest control and that the greatest care is taken of all the war property of Soviet Russia.

Instructions to Regimental Commissars

(1) The duties of all other Commissars attached to the army, including the Regimental Commissars, are the same as those of the Army Commissars, and all instructions to the latter apply equally to them.

(2) A Regimental Commissar should be always at the side of the officer commanding the regiment for the following purposes:

(a) He must be present when orders are received and when verbal orders are given and verbal arrangements made.

(b) He must accompany the officer commanding the regiment when he inspects any regimental units.

(c) He must be always at the commanding officer's side when the regiment goes into action. He must watch the course of operations, encourage his own attacking or defending troops and set them an example by taking a personal part in the engagement, when necessary.

(3) A Commissar must watch the regimental commander's activities from a political point of view, but must not interfere with the latter's purely operative actions.

(4) A Commissar gives validity to all the commanding officer's orders by appending his signature to them and must see that no orders are issued without his signature.

(5) A Regimental Commissar organizes, directs and supervises the political work in his regiment. He has the assistance of a political leader, who organizes all the political work in the regiment.

(6) With the aid of his assistant the Regimental Commissar directs and supervises all departments of the regimental staff. He obtains, procures and manages all the supplies needed by the regiment.

(7) When on duty at the front, he is represented by his assistant.

(8) The Regimental Commissar's assistant must always be with the regiment's staff. All transport and all supplies are under his charge.

Scheme for the Transition to the Militia System

(1) The approaching end of the Civil War and the favourable change in the international situation of Soviet Russia make it necessary for us to remodel our military forces in accordance with the country's urgent economic and cultural needs.

(2) On the other hand it is necessary to affirm that the Socialist Republic can by no means be regarded as out of danger so long as the imperialist bourgeoisie holds the reins of government in the most important countries in the world.

The imperialists are losing ground, and at any moment the course of events may impel them to undertake further warlike adventures against Soviet Russia. Hence the necessity for maintaining the defences of the Revolution at the required standard.

(3) The transition period, which may be long and wearisome, must effect a reorganization of the armed forces which will give the workers the necessary military training while withdrawing them from productive labour as little as possible. Only a Militia of Red Workers and Peasants, based on the territorial system, can conform to these requirements.

(4) The essence of the Soviet militia system must be the closest possible association of the army with the processes of production, so that the man-power of certain defined industrial areas will also form the man-power of certain defined military units.

(5) The militia formations (regiments, brigades, divisions) must be territorially adapted to the territorial distribution of industry in such a way as will permit the industrial centres and their surrounding agricultural belts to constitute the bases of the militia formations.

(6) The organization of the Workers' and Peasants' Militia must be based on cadres well equipped in all military, technical and political respects to serve the needs of the workers and peasants continually trained by them. These cadres must be able at any given moment to call up the workers and peasants from their militia district, incorporate them in the military machine, arm them and take them into action.

(7) The transition to the militia system must take place gradually, in conformity with the military and international-diplomatic situation of the Soviet Republic, and under conditions which will not allow the defence strength of the Soviet Republic to fall below the necessary standard for even a single moment.

(8) When the gradual demobilization of the Red Army takes place, the best cadres must be stationed in the localities where they will be of greatest use, i.e., where they can best be adapted to local production conditions and modes of life, in order to ensure complete functioning of the administrative machinery of the militia formations.

(9) Renewals of the personnel of the militia cadres must take place gradually and in such a way as to ensure the closest contact with the economic life of the district in question, so that the commanding officers of a division stationed in a territory which comprises, for example, a mining area surrounded by a belt of villages, may be drawn from the best elements of the local proletariat.

(10) For the purpose of the aforesaid cadre renewals the courses to be taken by such officers must take place in localities most convenient to the requirements of the economic militia districts. Such courses must be taken by the best representatives of the local workers and peasants.

(11) The military training based on the militia system

which ensures the greatest fighting efficiency of a militia
army consists of the following:

(a) Preliminary training before the age of liability to
service. This involves the close co-operation of
the military authorities with the People's Commissariat for Education, Trade Unions, Party
Organizations, Youth Associations, Sports
Clubs, etc.

(b) Training of citizens who have reached the age of
liability. The duration of the training periods
should be continually shortened with ever-
increasing approximation of the barracks to a
political-military school.

(c) Short periods of repetitive training, for the purpose of testing the fighting efficiency of the
militia formations.

(12) The militia cadre organizations charged with the
duty of national defence must be adapted in such
measure as may be necessary to labour service, i.e., they
must be capable of forming labour squads and providing them with the necessary instructors.

(13) Since the militia must develop in the direction
of a nation of armed communists, its organizations
must retain during the present period all the characteristics of the dictatorship of the working classes.

(Approved by the 9th Congress of the Communist
Party of Russia, March 29–April 4, 1920.)

Appendix 11

CHRONICLE OF THE CIVIL WAR
First Period
November 1917–April 1918

Don Area
1917

Nov. 25—Ataman Kaledin's forces take the offensive, capture Rostov and shoot the captured Bolshevist members of the Rostov Soviet of Workers' Delegates.

Dec. (early)—Generals Kornilov, Alexiev, Denikin, and Markov escape from captivity in the Bychov prison and reach the Don area, where they begin to organize the White Volunteer Army.

Dec. 11–12—First engagements at Yusovka between Kaledin's forces and Red Guard formations.

1918

Jan. 28—Red Army under Sivers captures Taganrog. Red Army under Sablin and Petrov captures the Kamenka railway-station.

Feb. 24—The Reds take Rostov. The White Volunteers retreat on Kuban.

The Ukraine
1918

Jan. 16—The Revolutionary Committee gain possession of Kiev after victorious street fighting.

Jan. 16—Red troops enter Kiev and effect a junction with the rebel garrison.

Feb.—German advance into the Ukraine.

Mar.—Capture of Kiev by the Germans and allied Ukrainians.

April 7—Evacuation of Kharkov. The entire Ukraine remains occupied by German and Austrian troops until the end of May. The *Rada* Government rules under their protection, but is driven out later by Hetman Skoropadsky.

Second Period

May 1918–beginning of 1920

1918

May—The Czechoslovak Legion revolts and occupies the middle Volga area.

Sept. 8—Red forces take the offensive against the Czechoslovaks and White irregulars.

Sept. 10—The Reds capture Kazan.

Sept. 12—The 1st Red Army, commanded by Tuchachevsky, captures Simbirsk.

Oct. 7—Red forces enter Samara and receive a ceremonial welcome from revolting workers.

Dec. 12—Fall of Ufa.

1919

Jan. 22—Red forces break the enemy's obstinate resistance when fighting in 30 degrees of frost and take Orenburg.

Feb. 27—Fall of Orsk and complete annihilation of White regulars. Kolchak raises an army in Siberia to take their place.

Mar.—Admiral Kolchak takes the offensive.

Apr. 12—Kolchak advances to within 30 versts east of the Volga.

May 4—Battle of Busuluk. The Red Army commanded by Tuchachevsky takes Bugurslan.

May 27—The Reds take Orenburg.

June 10—The Reds take Ufa.

Aug. 3—The Reds take Chelyabinsk, with 15,000 prisoners, and annihilate three divisions of Kolchak's army.

Sept.—Under pressure of the enemy who has taken the offensive, Red forces retreat to the River Tobol.

Nov. 14—Fall of Omsk.

Dec. 15—Fall of Novo-Nikolayevsk, now known as Novo-Sibirsk.

Dec. 29—Capture of Tomsk, along with many prisoners, including the general staff and all other staffs.

1920

Jan.—Fall of Krasnoyarsk. The enemy's last remaining forces capitulate.

Turkestan

After the annihilation of Kolchak's army the Turkestan front came into existence in August 1919.

1920

Jan. 5—Capture of the town of Gurev, the base of the Ural Cossacks.
Feb. 18—Red forces take Khiva.

The Ukraine

From April to November 1918, Red forces occupied the line of demarcation. In December Red troops began a general attack on the Ukraine front.

1919

Jan. 3—The Reds take Kharkov.
Jan. 20—Poltava captured after fighting of sixteen hours' duration.
Feb. 5—Ukraine Soviet forces capture Kiev. Petliura's Directory in flight.
Mar. 11—Soviet troops take Kherson.
May—Red troops, advancing all along the line from Odessa to the Crimea, reach the Black Sea.

The Struggle Against Denikin
1919

Spring—General Denikin takes the offensive with volunteer armies of Don and Caucasian troops.
May 26—White Volunteers take Kharkov.

Middle of August—Red forces taken the offensive on the southern front. Their initial success is soon offset by a White counter-offensive.

Sept. 18—White Volunteers take Kursk.

Oct. 13—White volunteers take Orel.

Oct. 15—Red Army takes Kiev.

Second half of October—Red Armies of the southern front start an offensive in the direction of Orlov.

Nov. 17—The Red Army takes Kursk.

Dec. 12—The Red Army takes Kharkov and Poltava, Denikin's forces in hasty retreat on Rostov.

The Western Front
1918

December—The Lettish and Estonian Revolutionary Armies take the offensive, with the assistance of Russian western front formations, utilizing the withdrawal of German forces, now commencing, as an opportunity to advance.

Nov. 25—Pskov captured by Soviet forces.

Nov. 28—Narva captured.

Dec. 24—Yuryev and Vendek captured.

1919

March—Red forces reach the Baltic Sea.

April—Beginning of attacks by the enemy, who advances on Riga and Vilna with troops equipped with material provided by the Entente.

April to July—Fierce engagements of the scanty Red forces with better equipped and numerically superior opponents. The Reds evacuate Vilna and Latvia.

September—General Yudenich makes his first attack.

Oct. 11—Beginning of General Yudenich's second series of operations.

Oct. 23—Beginning of the Red counter-attacks which end with Yudenich's complete defeat.

Nov. 14—Yamburg taken.

January to December 1920
Northern Front
1920

Feb. 21—Archangelsk taken. General Miller's White Government of the North flies to the Arctic Ocean.

Feb. 26—Onega taken.

Mar. 14—Murmansk taken. 6 tanks, 89 engines and more than 1,000 wagons captured.

Western Front
1920

January to March—Peace negotiations and inactivity.

Mar. 6—Sudden outbreak of hostilities with Poland.

May 6—The Poles take Kiev.

May 14—The Red Army opens a general offensive in Polessiy–Lepel sector.

June 6—Budyonny's cavalry take Zhitomir and Berdichev.

June 12—The Red Army takes Kiev.

June 25—The Red Cavalry takes Brody.

July 4—The Red Army commanded by Tuchachevsky takes the offensive between the Beresina and the northern Dvina.

July 14—The Red Army takes Vilna.

July 19—The Red Army takes Grodno.

Aug. 1—Capture of Bialystok. Bielsk and Brest-Litovsk.

Aug. 13—The Red Cavalry takes Soldau.

Aug. 16—Fighting takes place 15 kilometres from Warsaw.

Aug. 15 and 16—Beginning of the Polish counter-offensive in the Warsaw, Ivangorod and Lublin sectors.

Aug.—Retreat of the Army of the Western Front. Its right wing is interned in East Prussia.

Aug. 15–20—Budyonny's Cavalry Army in action at Lwow.

Oct. 5—Red forces retreat to the line Lake Paroch–Smorgon–Minsk.

Oct. 5–12—Armistice.

Oct. 18—Retreat of our forces to the present frontier line and cessation of hostilities with Poland.

Petliura's Ukrainian Army was finally liquidated in the course of September and interned in Galicia.

January to March 1920
1920

Jan.—A series of indecisive actions with Denikin's troops on the Caucasus front.

Beginning of March—Red forces take the offensive in the Caucasus.

Mar. 2—Red Army captures Azov.

Mar. 17—Capture of Tiflis, Pyatigorsk, Armavir and Ekaterinodar.

Mar. 27—Capture of Novorossiisk.

Mar. 28—Capture of Baku.

May 4—The remnants of the Denikin forces driven to the Black Sea coast.

The Campaign against Wrangel
1920

Mar. 9—Red troops take the enemy's fortified lines at Yushunie and the Sivashky bridge, but retreat northward under enemy pressure.

April 13—Latvian Red forces repulsed in their attack on Perekop, in the Crimea.

June 6—Wrangel advances from the Crimea.

Sept.—Wrangel attacks the Don Basin.

Sept. 6—Wrangel's forces cross to the right bank of the Dnieper.

Oct. 14—Red Cavalry annihilate three enemy cavalry divisions and two infantry divisions at Pokrovsky. The enemy flee in panic. The beginning of the end for Wrangel.

Nov. 3—Red troops reach the Strait of Kerch.

Nov. 7–11—Red forces break through the enemy's fortified positions at Perekop and Taganash.

Nov. 11—Capture of Simferopol and Feodosia.

Nov. 15—Capture of Sevastopol.

Eastern Front
1920

January to March—Fall of Irkutsk. Kolchak and his ministers taken prisoners.

Oct. 21—Capture of Chita. The remnants of General Semyonov's forces withdraw to Manchuria.

Turkestan

Sept. 1—All Turkestan occupied. Conclusion of operations against Old Bokhara. Capture of the town by Red Bokhara forces. The Emir placed on the throne by the English flees to the mountains.

Third Period
1921

Feb. 26—Red Georgian rebels, assisted by Red troops, from the Soviet Republic of Azerbaijan, capture Tiflis.

Mar. 3—Outbreak of the Kronstadt Mutiny.

Mar. 17—Liquidation of the Kronstadt Mutiny.

Oct. 25—Capture of Vladivostok.

Bibliography

There is an extremely wide range of literature dealing with this subject; memoirs and reminiscences are particularly numerous. Research is, however, difficult, owing to the fact that Stalin's censorship has destroyed many of these works, while, with the exception of propagandist literature which possesses no historical value, no comprehensive works dealing with the Red Army and the Civil War have yet been written in any language. The Russian journals *Archives of the Proletarian Revolution* and *Red Archives* may be said to furnish important information.

As no comprehensive bibliography has yet been published in any language, I mention only the most essential reference works.

ANISHEV, A.: *A Study of the History of the Civil War*, 1917–20. Leningrad, 1925. (In Russian only.)

ANTONOV–OVSEYENKO: *Der Aufbau der Roten Armee in der Revolution*. Hamburg, 1923. Verlag Carl Heym, Nachfolger.

AVALOV, GENERAL PRINCE: *Im Kampfe gegen den Bolshewismus*. Hamburg, 1923. Verlag Albrecht von Egidy.

BENES, EDWARD: *My War Memories*. Allen and Unwin, 1928.

BUBNOV: *The Civil War; Parties and Military Problems.* Moscow, 1928. (In Russian only.)

Bürgerkrieg, Die illustrierte Geschichte des russischen. Berlin, 1928. Neuer deutscher Verlag. Published by J. Thomas.

The Civil War, 1918–21. Three volumes, edited by S. Kamenev, A. Bubnov, R. Eydemann. Moscow, 1928. (In Russian only.)

CHURCHILL, WINSTON: *The World Crisis,* 1916–8. Thornton Butterworth, 1923–31.

DENIKIN, GENERAL A. N.: *Umrisse der russischen Wirren.* Paris and Berlin, 1921–5. Five volumes. Verlag J. Powolotzki and Verlag "Slowo."

GUSSEV: *The Civil War and the Red Army.* Moscow, 1925. (In Russian only.)

Die Lehren des Bürgerkrieges. Hamburg, 1923. Verlag Carl Heym, Nachf.

HOFFMANN, MAJOR-GENERAL MAX: *Der Krieg der versamten Gelegenheiten.* Munich, 1924. Verlag für Kulturpolitik.

KAKURIN. *The Fighting in the Revolution.* Published by the War Academy, Moscow. 1925–6. (In Russian only.)

KERENSKY: *The Catastrophe.* D. Appleton & Co., New York and London.

Koltchak's Last Days. Materials edited by M. Konstantinov. Moscow, 1926. (In Russian only.)

KRITZMANN, L.: *The Heroic Period of the Russian Revolution.* Moscow, 1926. (In Russian only.)

KRYLENKO, N.: *Red and White Terror.* Published by the Communist Party of Great Britain. London, 1928.

LAVROV, P.: *The Paris Commune.* Zurich, 1880. (In Russian only.)

LENIN: *Collected Works.* Martin Lawrence, 1927. A study of Vols. VIII, XVI, XX, XXI, XXII, XXIII, XXV, and XXVI is advisable.
Oktoberrevolution und Rote Armee. Berlin, 1932. Internationaler Arbeiterverlag.

LEVIDOV: *History of the Entente Intervention in Russia.* Leningrad, 1925. (In Russian only.)

MARTY, ANDRÉ: *La Révolte de la Mer Noire.* Paris, 1927. Bureau d'Edition, de Diffusion et de Publicité.

MASARYK, T. G.: *The Making of a State.* Allen and Unwin, 1927.

MILYUTIN: *The Economic Organization of Soviet Russia.* Published by the Communist Party of Great Britain. London, 1931.

REISSNER, LARISSA: *Oktober.* Berlin, 1927. Neuer deutscher Verlag.

PILSUDSKI, JOSEPH: *The Memoirs of a Polish Revolutionary and Soldier.* Faber & Faber, 1931.

PRICE, MORGAN PHILIPS: *My Reminiscences of the Russian Revolution.* Allen and Unwin, 1921.

PUTNA: *Before Warsaw.* Moscow, 1923. (In Russian only.)

The Revolutionary War Soviet of the U.S.S.R. for Ten Years. Moscow, 1928. (In Russian only.)

Revolution, Illustrierte Geschichte der russischen. Edited by W. Astrov, A. Slepkov, J. Thomas. Berlin, 1928. Neuer deutscher Verlag.

Rote Armee, Die: Ein Sammelbuch mit Beiträgen von S. Kamenev, L. Trotzki, K. Radek u.a. Vienna, 1923. Verlag für Literatur und Politik.

SERGEYEV: *From the Dvina to the Vistula.* Petrograd, 1923. (In Russian only.)

STALIN: *Problems of Leninism.* International Publishers, New York, 1934.

The October Revolution. Martin Lawrence, 1934.

TROTSKY: *Between Red and White.* Published by the Communist Party of Great Britain. London, 1922.

Der Geburt der Roten Armee. Vienna, 1924. Verlag für Literatur und Politik.

How the Revolution Armed. Moscow, 1923–5. (In Russian only.)

Fälschung der Geschichte der russischen Revolution. Berlin, 1928. Verlag Volkswille.

TUCHACHEVSKY: *The Class War.* Petrograd, 1921. (In Russian only.)

The Red Army and the Militia. Petrograd, 1921. (In Russian only.)

The March across the Vistula. Lectures delivered at the Complementary Course of the War Academy, Moscow, Feb. 7–10, 1923. (In Russian only.)

WRIGHT, CAPTAIN PETER: *At the Supreme War Council.* Eveleigh Nash, 1921.

Index

Marty, 101
Marx, Karl, 3, 15, 85
May Executions, the, 218
Mechonoshin, 74
Medical Commission, the, 175
Medlin, 132
Medvedyev,"Marshal Forward,"
    83
Menshevists, the, 20, 22, 26
Military Commission, the, 17, 175
Military Doctrine, 78, 200
Military Oath, the, 177, 178
Miller, General, 99
Ministry of War, 75
Minsk, 165, 190
Monarchist Parties, the, 118
Morgan, J. Pierpont, 188
Moscow, 10, 18, 22, 26, 35, 37,
    42, 80, 94, 95, 96, 100,
    102, 103, 107, 118, 119,
    165, 166, 185, 192, 218,
    226, 228, 234, 237, 238,
    242, 245
Mosyrz, 122, 128, 133
Mukden, 142
Muklevitch, 124
Muraviov, Colonel M. A., 67,
    68, 82, 91
Murmansk, 89, 92, 99

N
Napoleon, 97, 200
Napoleon's Egyptian Campaign,
    197
Narodniks, 32
Narva, the, 9
National Guard, the, 53
Natural Produce Tax, the, 112,
    119
"N.C.O. Clique," the, 39
New Economic Policy, the
    (NEP), 119, 212
Nicholas, Tsar, 14
Nikitin, 25
Niklyndov, 67
Nikolayev, General, 64
Noske, 19
November Revolution in Ger-
    many and Austro-Hun-
    gary, the, 93

Novo-Nikolayevsk, 88
Novorossiisk, 98

O
Ob, the, 88
October Revolution, the, 2, 6,
    16, 20, 28, 50, 55, 59, 67,
    74, 77, 78, 79, 80, 87, 89,
    114, 143, 151, 152, 163,
    217, 222, 223, 231
Okopnaya Pravda, 18
Omsk, 96, 107
On Military Doctrine, 123, 145
On Trotskyism, 151
Ordyonikidse, 166
Orel, 94, 97
Orenburg, Steppes the, 83
Ossovetz, 130

P
Paris, 238
Paris Commune, the, 52, 53
Paris Commune, the, 52
Party Day, the 10th, 118
Pepov, 149
Perekop, 165
Petersburg, St., 59
Petersburg Technical School, the,
    164
Petliura, 101
Petrograd, 10, 11, 17, 18, 21, 22,
    23, 24, 25, 34, 41, 42, 67,
    77, 80, 89, 98, 114, 115, 151
  Military Commission, 18
*Petrograd Workers' and Soldiers'
    News*, 22
Petrov, 84
Petrovsky, General, 241, 242
Piatakov, Georgi, 7, 57, 81, 86,
    124, 193, 214, 215, 222,
    239, 242
  Leonid, 86
Pilsudski, 63, 121, 122, 123, 125,
    126, 127, 128, 129, 130,
    131, 132, 133, 135, 136,
    137, 138, 142, 144, 145,
    196, 197
Pishpek, 164
Podvoisky, 25
Poland, 5, 100, 101, 121, 126,
    134, 144, 148

282

THE RED ARMY

Society for Air and Chemical
  Defence, the, 181
Sokolnikov, 8, 223, 237
Soldatskaya Pravda, 18
Sosnovski, General, 132
Soviet Government, the, 7, 15,
  16, 19, 37, 39, 42, 43, 54,
  59, 62, 64, 67, 68, 80, 83,
  87, 88, 90, 96, 140, 149,
  170, 227, 240, 246
  Union, the, 2, 15, 42, 66, 128,
    149, 203, 204, 205, 209,
    211, 212, 216, 217, 223,
    224, 225, 227, 231, 238,
    239, 244
Spain, 19, 247
Spree, the, 147
Stalin, Josef, 8, 57, 86, 91, 124,
  125, 134, 135, 136, 138,
  139, 147, 149, 150, 151,
  152, 164, 165, 166, 167,
  168, 189, 202, 205, 208,
  210, 213, 214, 215, 217,
  218, 219, 224, 225, 226,
  237, 239, 241, 242, 243,
  246, 247
Stassova, 8
Steklov, 13
Stefanik, General, 88
Sternberg, Baron Ungern, 100
Stockholm, 164, 167
Stupochenko, L., 11
Sutshan, 30, 32
Sverdlov, 8, 11, 12
Sviyazhsk, 91, 152, 153, 154, 156
Switzerland, 55
Szepycky, General, 129

T
Taganrog, 97, 107
Taiga, the, 29, 33
Tallinn, 134
Tannenberg, Battle of, 140, 141
Ten Theses of Soviet Power, 169
Territorial Army, the, 174, 175,
  176, 177
The Advance beyond the Vistula,
  126
*The Collapse of the Second
  International*, 229
The First Cavalry Army, 185

The Red Army and the Militia,
  171
The Year 1920, 126
Third Revolution, the, 117
Tikhoryetsk, 98
Tomsk, 96
Tomsky, 210, 223, 239
Trans-Siberian Railway, the, 87,
  88
Troika, the, 164, 166
Trotsky, L. D., 10, 20, 23, 24, 37,
  38, 39, 40, 41, 46, 51, 57,
  60, 63, 64, 66, 70, 72, 78,
  81, 90, 91, 97, 98, 101,
  110, 123, 138, 145, 149,
  150, 151, 152, 153, 154,
  155, 156, 157, 158, 159,
  160, 161, 162, 163, 164,
  168, 169, 173, 178, 189,
  190, 192, 197, 198, 201,
  205, 209, 218, 234, 235,
  237, 238, 239, 241
Trotsky and the Red Army, 62
Trotsky, Organiser of Victory,
  158
Tsarist Army, the, 3, 16, 19, 46,
  63, 72, 73, 74, 106
  Officers, 40, 46, 56, 66, 67, 68,
    71, 72, 73, 99, 151, 159,
    189, 220
  Russia, 5
Tuchachevsky, M. N., 39, 57, 59,
  60, 61, 62, 68, 91, 95, 96,
  98, 106, 118, 124, 125,
  126, 127, 128, 129, 130,
  131, 132, 133, 134, 135,
  136, 137, 138, 139, 140,
  142, 143, 144, 145, 169,
  171, 173, 177, 190, 191,
  192, 193, 194, 195, 196,
  197, 198, 199, 200, 201,
  209, 210, 211, 212, 214,
  215, 216, 218, 224, 226,
  230, 233, 236, 237, 238,
  239, 240, 241, 242, 243,
  246, 247
Tula Military Circuit, the, 125
Turkestan, 96, 165, 240
Turkey, 100
Turkmenistan, 212